SHOCK-SHIFT IN AN ENLARGED EUROPE

Shock-Shift in an Enlarged Europe

The geography of socio-economic change in East-Central Europe after 1989

Edited by

F.W. CARTER
Department of Social Sciences
School of Slavonic and East European Studies, University of London

and

W. MAIK
Department of Social Geography and Tourism
Nicholas Copernicus University, Toruń

Routledge
Taylor & Francis Group
LONDON AND NEW YORK

First published 1999 by Ashgate Publishing

Reissued 2018 by Routledge
2 Park Square, Milton Park, Abingdon, Oxon, OX14 4RN
711 Third Avenue, New York, NY 10017, USA

Routledge is an imprint of the Taylor & Francis Group, an informa business

A Library of Congress record exists under LC control number: 98074443

ISBN 13: 978-1-138-35206-3 (hbk)
ISBN 13: 978-0-429-43490-7 (ebk)

Contents

List of Figures vii
List of Tables viii
List of Contributors ix
Acknowledgements xi

1 Introduction
F. W. Carter and W. Maik 1

2 Transformations and Dilemmas of the Polish Economy
Zbyszko Chojnicki, Teresa Czyż and Jerzy J. Parysek 7

3 Geographical Aspects of Societal Transformation in the Czech Republic
Martin Hampl and Jan Müller 27

4 Some Features and Problems of the Transformation Process in Slovakia
Ján Paulov 39

5 Recent Changes in the Socio-Economic Structure of Slovenia
Marijan M. Klemenčić 49

6 The Resurgence of Submerged Minorities: Hungarians and Italians in Slovenia
André-Louis Sanguin 61

7 Industrial Restructuring Through Privatization: Evidence from Romania
Claudia Popescu 71

8 Restructuring of Urban and Rural Settlement in Estonia
A. Marksoo 81

9 The Transformation of Polish Retailing
Andrzej Werwicki 103

10 The Process of Socio-Economic Change in East-Central Europe after 1989: A View from Western Europe
Andrew H. Dawson 107

11 Environmental Geopolitics and Shock-Shift Transition in the Czech Republic
Andrew Tickle 113

12 The Prospects for Slovenia: Some Opportunities and Constraints
John Sargent 123

13 Which Transition? Some Thoughts on 'Some Features and Problems of the Transformation Process in Slovakia' by Ján Paulov
Adrian Smith 131

14 Privatization in Romania, with Particular Reference to the Rural Areas
David Turnock 137

15 Albania, Macedonia and Bulgaria: A Belt of Opportunity and Instability
George Prévélakis 153

16 The Restructuring of Urban and Rural Settlement in Estonia: A Comment
Tim Unwin 159

17 Regional Change in Russia: New Scales, New Issues, New Actors
M. J. Bradshaw 169

18 Conclusion
F. W. Carter and W. Maik 181

List of Figures

Figure 2.1 Strong, average and weak regions in Poland, 1986 19
Figure 3.1 Basic characteristics of geographical differentiation of transformation changes in the Czech Republic 35
Figure 3.2 Regional pattern of unemployment in the Czech Republic (31 August 1993) 36
Figure 3.3 Income tax from employees and small entrepreneurs (in Czech crowns, per capita, January–September 1993) 37
Figure 4.1 Slovakia: unemployment rate in the former large administrative units (December 1990–February 1994) 42
Figure 4.2 Slovakia: unemployment rate, 31 January 1993 43
Figure 8.1a Urban system of Estonia: hierarchical-functional structure 101
Figure 8.1b Urban system of Estonia: core and periphery 102
Figure 16.1 The capitalist market economy and 'place' 164

List of Tables

Table 2.1	Poland: classification of regions, 1992	23
Table 3.1	Selected characteristics of geographical differentiation of transformation changes in the Czech Republic	31
Table 4.1	Slovakia: selected macro-economic indicators	40
Table 4.2	Slovakia: basic indicators of national economic development	41
Table 5.1	Regional structure of Slovenian imports in 1992 (%)	52
Table 5.2	Regional structure of Slovenian exports in 1991 and 1992 (%)	52
Table 5.3	Slovenia: number of workers employed in industry and their share of the active population	53
Table 5.4	The development of urbanization in Slovenia	57
Table 7.1	Romania: share of the active population employed in industry, 1990–92	75
Table 8.1	Estonian settlement system in 1989	85
Table 8.2	Ethnic aspect of the employment structure of Estonia in 1989	86
Table 8.3	Shifts in the dynamics of Estonian urban population	87
Table 8.4	Estonia: redistribution of employees in basic spheres of activity (formal economy)	90
Table 8.5	Changes in the employment and functional structure of Estonian urban settlements (1990–94)	91
Table 8.6	Dynamics of the private farms in Estonia	92
Table 8.7	Estonia: changes in employment structure of rural population	94
Table 8.8	Estonia: dynamics of rural population by patterns of settlements in 1989–94	96
Table 8.9	Estonia: extent of concentration in rural settlement in 1995	97
Table 14.1	Migration in seven Carpathian districts, 1986–93	144
Table 14.2	Summary profiles of seven Carpathian districts	146

List of Contributors

M. J. Bradshaw
School of Geography, University of Birmingham

F. W. Carter
Dept of Social Sciences, School of Slavonic and East European Studies, University of London

Zbyszko Chojnicki
Institute of Socio-Economic Geography and Spatial Planning, Adam Mickiewicz University, Poznań

Teresa Czyż
Institute of Socio-Economic Geography and Spatial Planning, Adam Mickiewicz University, Poznań

Andrew H. Dawson
Dept of Geography, University of St Andrews

Martin Hampl
Dept of Social Geography, Charles University, Prague

Marijan M. Klemenčić
Dept of Geography, Ljubljana University

W. Maik
Dept of Social Geography and Tourism, Nicholas Copernicus University, Toruń

A. Marksoo
Institute of Geography, University of Tartu

Jan Müller
Dept of Social Geography, Charles University, Prague

Jerzy J. Parysek
Institute of Socio-Economic Geography and Spatial Planning, Adam Mickiewicz University, Poznań

Ján Paulov
Dept of Regional Geography, Landscape Protection and Planning, Comenius University, Bratislava

Claudia Popescu
Institute of Geography, Romanian Academy of Sciences, Bucharest

George Prévélakis
Institute of Geography, University of Paris-IV, Paris

André-Louis Sanguin
Dept of Geography, University of Angers

John Sargent
Dept of Geography, School of Oriental and African Studies, University of London

Adrian Smith
School of Social Sciences, University of Sussex

Andrew Tickle
Centre for Extra-Mural Studies, Birkbeck College, University of London

David Turnock
Dept of Geography, University of Leicester

Tim Unwin
Dept of Geography, Royal Holloway College, University of London

Andrzej Werwicki
Institute of Economic Geography and Spatial Organization, University of Łódź

Acknowledgements

The editors would like to thank the British Academy for a grant towards the production of camera-ready copy for this book, and John Andrew for his sterling work in completing this vital task. During our stay in Poland the generous hospitality offered by the Geographical Institute at the Nicholas Copernicus University in Toruń is gratefully acknowledged, together with the warmth and friendliness of officials at Toruń County Hall, the Mayor and his colleagues at Toruń City Hall, and staff at the Regional Centre for the Study and Protection of the Cultural Environment in that city. We should also like to acknowledge the efforts made by British colleagues from the conference for their help in improving the linguistic presentation of some of the texts. Finally, Professor Hampl and Dr Müller would like to acknowledge the receipt of financial support from the Czech Grant Agency (Grant Number 205/93/0823) which enabled them to carry out research for their chapter.

1 Introduction

F. W. CARTER and W. MAIK

This book is devoted to a geographical analysis of problems associated with socio-economic changes taking place in East-Central Europe. These problems have resulted from the demise of the Communist order and transition of these countries to a market economy and a democratic system. The idea behind this volume is to provide a confrontation of two viewpoints — the major chapters are written by East European scholars, followed by discussions held with their Western European counterparts.The idea was to provide depth and clarity to the debate on understanding those geographical problems facing the emerging East European states nearly a decade after the fall of the Iron Curtain.

The volume results from contributions made by colleagues at a geographical conference held in Toruń, Poland, in late 1994.[1] A summary of the content of these papers written by East European colleagues highlighted the regional imbalance found in Poland, the Czech Republic and Slovakia through papers by Zbyszko Chojnicki and his colleagues, Martin Hampl and Ján Paulov, with the most vigourous changes found in these countries' western regions and metropolitan areas. Claudia Popescu discovered that in Romania the more developed industrial regions had witnessed a more vibrant privatization process giving them an enhanced economic status over the rest of the country. Regional growth centres and the significance of southern rural fringe areas were seen as meaningful in both Estonia (A. Marksoo) and Slovenia (Marijan M. Klemenčić). A tendency towards agglomeration was clearly visible in Estonian towns such as Narva, Pärnu and Tartu, largely resulting from the vulnerability of local rural centres to agricultural privatization and the demise of giant farm organizations formerly linked to extensive rural centres. In Slovenia, programmes aimed at revitalizing underdeveloped zones were being undertaken through infrastructural investment and attempts at rejuvenating social organization.

Input from West European colleagues clearly emphasized the role of the regional dimension. It was apparent to them that regions in Eastern Europe varied immensely. This was evident when considering not only the economic base, but also settlement patterns and overall infrastructure. Moreover, regional differences also resulted from political influence, which wielded considerable power over attempts at restructuring, the creation of small businesses and inducements for foreign direct investment. In turn these factors had contributed to specific regional problems. For example, in Romania (David Turnock), and Estonia (Tim Unwin), it was clear that a process of reversal from the former large state farm to small family farms was beginning to have an impact on the structure of rural areas. There was also a clear demand for an appreciation of the environmental dimension in regional studies (Andrew Tickle). Problems associated with ethnicity were also emphasized. A clarion call for a better understanding of Balkan society, necessary if we are to comprehend the ethnic quarrels that occur in this part of our continent, was made by George Prévélakis. The significance of ethnic minority status was also discussed by André-Louis Sanguin and John Sargent, using Slovenia as an example. A case for modelling the regional geography of transition was made by M. J. Bradshaw, in order to aid attempts at synthesizing the complexity of factors involved in the transition process. In turn, results from such work could provide a core of case-studies for further comparative work on the resulting performance and future potential of particular regional areas. Andrew H. Dawson summarized the differences in approach between advocates of an entirely self-regulating market system and one with significant government intervention.

Inevitably, a book based on conference papers suffers from lacunae relating to the overall theme. Here more could have been stated on theoretical and conceptual issues which are not covered systematically in this work. Moreover, except for the short paper by Andrzej Werwicki, there is little to offer on the significance of the retailing process; chapters on the role of transport and the importance of urban restructuring would also have added to the wider thematic and national/regional coverage of the shock-shift phenomenon. In spite of these shortcomings, it is an accepted fact that shock-shift has been imposed on the emerging countries of Eastern Europe and the civil societies in each state have had to discover ways of trying to come to terms with the new situation. Some are coping better than others with the demands for initiating new systems and institutions in spite of the unavoidable hold-ups caused by political debate and delayed decisions on resource allocation.

During the early 1990s the modernization-dependency model was being proposed by the European Community, and a significant number of other post-Communist societies/establishments, for heralding East-Central Europe's 'return to Europe'. If one disregards the intricate considerations of definition, it is understood that the modernization concept refers to a sequence of changes occurring in less-developed or semi-peripheral systems. It is influenced by contact with industrial or post-industrial civilizations which possess suitable technology as well as economic, political and social organization. Social development assumes transition from an industrial to post-industrial/informational phase, where progress has already reached this stage in the advanced civilizations of richer states.

Although we are in general agreement with this development, the following riders may be proposed. First, modernization should proceed at the microscale within local communities as well as at the macroscale of nation, state, or world system. In other words, local development is not an alternative to global processes but complimentary to them. The transformation process in post-Communist countries depends on modernization at the microscale, starting with innovation mechanisms at the local level. Secondly, development processes are very complex and not just influenced by external actions. An imported modernization programme can accelerate economic growth and social progress, but it can also have some serious side effects. For example, it can create inequality within the dynamics of a particular region, leading to the formation of isolated 'modernity enclaves'; it may also contribute to ecological degradation and produce feelings of social and individual deprivation amongst many groups and communities.

Thirdly, modernization based on imported technology, capital and organizational models usually (though not always) leads to asymmetric interdependence. This has many negative consequences, such as capital or technical dependence and asymmetry of political pressure. It fossilizes the division of labour between centre and periphery/semi-periphery, causing difficulties in the transition of individual countries from peripheral to central locations. Empirical analysis has shown that most countries usually reproduce their own situation rather than improve it.

These negative effects of modernizational development suggest a need for the re-evaluation of this model. Internal development factors should play a decisive part in this process, while external factors can only provide support and help catalyze it. A revision of the model should take change and the development process of a community into account. One may add that local communities and the most creative individuals in them are also subject to changes in this development process. Clearly the principle of rational eclectism is inherent in selectively combining the various assumptions of this development.

At this point it is perhaps important to stress that the post-Communist countries of East-Central Europe have proved of great interest to economic geographers. The legacy of a Soviet-imposed type of 'real socialism' appears to have been more fundamental and enduring in the region than was previously believed. Many of the immediate benefits and eventual changes emerging from the demise of the old system have yet to materialize and it is still not clear where they will lead us. Under such circumstances it is perhaps better to think in terms of a transformation from a known past to an unknown future, rather than transition to a guaranteed end-state.[2] We must also remind ourselves of the oft-forgotten fact that the West has experienced a very long period of brutal and sometimes cruel capitalism, which preceded later organization leading to a fairly successful attempt at establishing some degree of social control over the economy.

Many people in East-Central Europe wish to experience a rapid movement from 'real socialism' to a liberal democracy and capitalist market economy. Dahrendorf[3] maintained in 1990 that while Poland, Czechoslovakia and Hungary may reach some form of democratic constitution within six months, it would take a further six years before the benefits of liberal economic reform appeared and a staggering sixty years to obtain the sort of social framework and democratic constitutional order necessary for a market economy to establish itself within a vigorous civil society. Admittedly he later revised the latter period to a mere two generations.

Economic liberalization also has its dangers. According to Weitman,[4] this could lead to wider social inequalities and a need for state intervention, encouraging the return of state control. He also argued that rapid change could have dire consequences throughout society, leading to a steep increase in social problems, for example, widespread corruption, savage crimes, drug and alcohol abuse, truancy, juvenile delinquency, prostitution, suicide, mental illness and so on. Such effects could again lead to demands for state intervention.

In fact, Weitman contests that it is too idealistic to try and attempt to achieve spectacular results rapidly. However desirable in the short term the idea of liberal democracy and belief in a market economy could be, this invites failure and the risk of backlash. The revival of ex-Communists in Lithuania (an excessive example), and some other East European/former Soviet satellite states, combined with right-wing nationalism and a revival of antisemitism, provide us with some warning signs. Václav Klaus's determination to prove that the Czech Republic was already in a post-transformation phase perhaps proved a little premature. In fact, it was his neo-liberal economic policies that contributed to the Czech-Slovak split.[5]

Perhaps now eight years after the event, one can inquire whether shock therapy has been successful within the period claimed by its advocates. After all it was in Poland, where our initial conference took place, that the land of the first and probably most successful radical post-Communist reforms were created, composed of powerful and carefully balanced macroeconomic measures. It was this stimulating background that saw initial discussions and the eventual commital of thoughts to paper that has led to the appearance of this book.

Notes

1 D. Turnock, 'Shock-Shift in an Enlarged Europe: Socio-Economic Change in East-Central Europe since 1989', *GeoJournal*, vol. 34, no. 4, 1994, pp. 522–3.
2 C. G. A. Bryant and E. Mokrzycki (eds), *The New Great Transformation: Change and Continuity in East-Central Europe*, London and New York, 1994, p. i.
3 R. Dahrendorf, *Reflections on the Revolution in Europe*, London, 1990.
4 S. Weitman, 'Thinking the Revolutions of 1989', *British Journal of Sociology*, vol. 43, 1992, pp. 1–24.
5 V. Rey (ed.), *Transition, fragmentation, recomposition: La Tchéco-Slovaquie en 1992*, Fontenay-St. Cloud, 1994.

2 Transformations and Dilemmas of the Polish Economy

ZBYSZKO CHOJNICKI, TERESA CZYŻ and JERZY J. PARYSEK

The aim of this chapter is to outline the character of the transformation of the Polish economy and the dilemmas it involves. Naturally, this is neither a complete survey of issues, nor a summary of opinions on the matter. We hope, however, that it will contribute to a better understanding of the character of changes taking place in Poland and the state of its economy in the period of transition. The starting point is a discussion of four issues: (1) systemic changes taking place in Poland; (2) ways of restructuring the economy; (3) the state of the economy; and (4) regional differences in the restructuring of the economy.

The Character and Strategy of the Systemic Transformation

The systemic transformation taking place in Poland as well as in other post-Communist countries is an exceptional phenomenon, especially in its economic aspect. It is not a continuation of the course of development pursued hitherto, but a break from it; it proceeds on a new basis. In addition, it takes place under the conditions of a socio-economic crisis generated back in the 1980s which is a serious barrier to the pace and scope of systemic change in Poland (Chojnicki, 1990). Before passing on to this subject, let us present (1) the causes of the breakdown of the Communist system; (2) the strategy of the transformation; and finally (3) its dilemmas.

Causes of the Breakdown

The collapse of the Communist system in Poland in 1989 was preceded and determined by a number of events both on the domestic and international scenes. It is impossible here to weigh and assess them fully; this will be the task for historians.

Among endogenous factors which have brought about a global socio-economic crisis are the following:

(1) growing societal disquiet with the low standards of living and limited state independence, expressed in successive political upheavals undermining the regime and forcing attempts at reform: 1956 (Poznań), 1970 (the Coast), 1976 (Ursus and Radom), and 1980–81 (the principal national centres);

(2) changes in social consciousness, especially an increasingly critical attitude of the working class towards the supposedly progressive nature of the Communist system and its efficiency, and the formation of opposition organizations such as the Committee for Workers' Defence (KOR) and Solidarity;

(3) growing inefficiency and shortages in an economy based on central planning and the performance of state-run enterprises; their manifestations were: (a) an antiquated structure of the economy, a falling level of investment and a steady decrease in the value of *per capita* national property; (b) growing foreign debt; and (c) depleted resources of the natural environment.

Exogenous factors include, of course, the collapse of the military and political power of the former USSR, followed by its destabilization and disintegration as a result of the lost arms race and unsuccessful attempts at reforming that state.

The Scope and Path of Transformation

The systemic transformation has embraced both the main subsystems: political and economic. The radical reforms that have taken place in the world in the latter half of the twentieth century either consisted in the democratization of the political system (Spain in the late 1970s, South Korea in the late 1980s), or focused on the economic system (Mexico in recent years).

While changes in Poland were initiated in both systems at the same time, they have led to political transformation first: free elections, a multi-party system and a democratic mode of government and self-government formation. The classic sequence of development — first capitalism, then democracy — has been reversed.

It is assumed as a principle that the changes instituted in Poland should lead to the formation of a market or capitalist economy. The model of a market economy to be implemented has, however, not been precisely defined, despite some reflections offered on the subject. The question that arises at this point is whether we should look to the Western tradition of a market economy to supply the theoretical and empirical foundations of its model, or some universal conception (Krawczyk, 1990; Hübner, 1992).

In the pragmatic perspective, the way of transformation is more important than the target model. Neither the theory of economic development nor the history of development of the capitalist economy provide a basis for satisfactory theoretical directions for monitoring the process of the transformation.

The fundamental difference between the formation of the market economy in the West and in Poland is that the mechanisms which have developed in an evolutionary way in the former have to be introduced in Poland artificially, so to speak, through rapid legal-institutional changes, and that in a bad macro-economic situation, in particular under an acute structural crisis: much inefficient heavy industry, loss of former USSR markets, and low economic efficiency (cf. Kubin and Żekoński, 1992; Łukawer, 1994).

The choice of restructuring strategy for the Polish economy has played a part in the stabilization processes. Basically, there are two main strategies: (1) radical, and (2) of step-by-step changes.

The radical strategy, associated with and introduced by Balcerowicz, consisted of rapid and radical stabilization and liberalization and profound institutional reconstruction (Wilczyński et al., 1992). In practice, stabilization and liberalization preceded institutional transformation, which lessened their effects and led to a drop in production and a rise in unemployment.

The strategy of step-by-step changes has assumed different forms depending on the degree of stabilization and liberalization (of prices and foreign trade and so on).

The evaluation of these strategies is made from the point of view of the risk to the economy and the chances of reviving it.

The first stage, covering the years 1989–93, was dominated by radical transformation, which has led to:

- a decline in inflation,
- elimination of shortages,
- widening of the variety of goods and services offered,
- convertibility of the złoty,
- strengthening of the role of foreign trade,
- increased efficiency in the utilization of energy and materials,
- introduction of the categories of profit and marketing in the operation of enterprises, and
- privatization of trade and services as well as smaller manufacturing establishments.

The implementation of the transformation in its second stage requires profound institutional reconstruction. There are opinions, however, that the rate of these changes has slackened recently, as a result of disputes about the nature and scope of privatization after Pawlak's government had been formed in the second half of 1993.

Main Dilemmas of the Transformation

Dilemmas are generated by those aspects of the transformation which make it necessary to accommodate extra-economic considerations.

Social consent to reforms The introduction of political demo-cracy, maintaining the big role of trade unions (OPZZ, Solidarity), and growing societal discontent makes the social acceptance of the reforms the principal factor of change. Transformations of the macrosystem make sense only when they result from the will of the majority. A fundamental dilemma that arises at this point is the choice of such means and strategies as would reinforce the reformers and enable them to carry reforms into effect. The proof came with the parliamentary election in Poland in 1993, which was won by those parties in whose platforms the main plank was the reduction of costs society has to pay for the restructuring of the economy.

The role of the state in guiding market-oriented changes We should differentiate between the steering of transformation and the steering of the economy. In the former question, whatever the opinions on the spontaneous nature of change, it is clearly necessary for the state to set the direction of legal-institutional transformations. The short duration of successive governments in Poland does not help here, but on the other hand it allows each new administration to make corrections and respond to shifts in public opinion. The main line of change has, however, been maintained. As to the other matter, it concerns the scope of state intervention; it has increased this year, attracting sharp criticism from the opposition.

Privatization It is generally assumed that the privatization of state-owned enterprises is the main element of the transformation leading to the establishment of a market economy in Poland. This is so because it improves the efficiency of management and draws foreign investors, at the same time absolving the state from the responsibility for their performance and financial support in the face of a severe crisis of production in large enterprises. Therefore, the rate of privatization and the number of firms under privatization are treated as measures of the effectiveness of the transformation process.

Simultaneously, however, reservations are expressed about treating privatization as an absolute category and a panacea. The performance of some of the privatized enterprises is still not good: there are bankruptcies, and foreign investors try to convert the state monopoly into their own or to get rid of competitors. It is estimated that the risk involved in foreign investments is lower in state-run enterprises than in private ones, especially in the power and fuel industries.

Stabilization and liberalization The stabilization of the economy is a necessary condition of its efficient performance, but it is not synonymous with its transformation into a reformed market system; what is more, under certain conditions it may conflict with this aim when the economy is stabilized at a low equilibrium level. Hence stabilization and transformation strategies have to be co-ordinated. In the Poland of 1989, which was suffering from hyper-inflation and shortages, it was necessary to restore the market balance and stabilization. This was done through the decontrol of prices and foreign trade, bringing inflation down, and lifting restrictions on the setting up of enterprise.

The Restructuring of the Economy

Ultimate Goals of Restructuring: Government Programmes

The ultimate goal of government programmes of converting the old centrally planned economy into a market one was the institution of such structural-organizational changes in the stagnating Polish economy as would modernize its key sectors. The intermediate goals included: the acceleration of development of the private sector until it played a dominant role in the ownership structure; demonopolization and deconcentration of the existing economic structures; the abandoning of the administrative mode of steering the economy; the introduction of economic instruments for measuring the performance of economic agents; price decontrol; the opening of the economy and hence better access to raw materials and strengthening the role of export; the convertibility of the złoty on the home market; promoting foreign investments in Poland, and so on (*Poland Your Business Partner*, 1992; *Poland: The New Business Frontier*, 1992). Some of these goals had been accomplished by 1994.

Privatization and Private Enterprise

One of the basic tasks of the restructuring process is the privatization of the Polish economy, so far carried out in either of two ways: one involving capital (a state-run enterprise is transformed into a partnership with the Treasury and then offered for public sale), and one involving liquidation (a direct sale [or lease] of a bankrupt or tottering enterprise with its assets treated as the buyer's shares in the newly created company) (Lewandowski and Szomburg, 1990; *Poland Your Business Partner*, 1992). This unprecedented large-scale process, intended to be completed in a relatively short period of time and embracing many different economic agents, was started in 1990 with the sale of the first state enterprises. By the end of 1991, 260 of them had been sold, in one way or the other, and by the end of 1994 this figure climbed to 332 (or 5 per cent of the total). The shareholders of these newly privatized companies include such well-known foreign firms as Pepsi-Co, Henkel, Phillips, Unilever, Volkswagen and Gerber. The privatization programme allows for two other forms of this process, yet to be implemented: sectoral privatization (transferring particular economic sectors as wholes into private hands), and mass privatization (shares in large enterprises for all citizens).

The new legal regulations have brought about rapid growth in private enterprise, especially in trade and services, including such hitherto state-dominated sectors of the economy as banking, foreign travel and domestic tourism, residential construction and foreign trade. Private and community schools of all levels, even in higher education, have been founded, as well as kindergartens, doctors' consulting rooms and clinics. Nearly all retail trade and over 80 per cent of wholesale trade is in private hands. By the end of 1993 there were 1.7 million establishments of natural persons (94.2 per cent of all economic agents) and over 83,000 (4.4 per cent) commercial partnerships, as against 5,900 (0.3 per cent) state-run enterprises, 19,700 (1 per cent) co-operatives and 650 (0.03 per cent) municipal establishments. It should be kept in mind, however, that the vast majority of private economic agents are small establishments often employing between one and five persons.

The Currency System: The Money and Capital Markets

The economic transformation, especially privatization, required the creation of a capital market in Poland and, before that, a reconstruction of the currency and banking systems. The złoty was devaluated by 45 per cent in December 1989, and again by 17 per cent in May 1991. A floating exchange rate for the internally convertible złoty was introduced, related to the rate of the five principal foreign currencies (the US dollar, the pound sterling, the Deutschmark, the Swiss franc and the French franc). In 1990, to guarantee this internal convertibility, Western countries opened a line of stabilization credit to the amount of one billion US dollars, which had never been tapped.

The banking system was restructured and now consists of a central bank (the National Bank of Poland [NBP]) and a network of ninety-one commercial banks of various kinds, including specialist ones (*Poland Your Business Partner*, 1992). To stop an uncontrolled rise in wages a temporary tax was levied on any rise not justified by an increase in efficiency. In April 1990 the Warsaw Stock Exchange opened with the offer for sale of shares of the first five companies (at the end of August 1994 there were thirty-three companies whose shares were officially quoted at the exchange, including twenty-eight on the primary market).

The Business Environment

Rapid development can also be observed as far as institutions of the business environment are concerned: the ninety-one commercial banks mentioned above, with their 3,500 customer-service branches in 1994, chambers of commerce and industry, economic chambers, business and innovation centres, economic foundations, enterprise incubators, business-support foundations and private schools of business, marketing, banking and so on. Their number and nature are largely determined by local initiatives as well as by the intellectual potential of voivodeships, towns and communes. A big role is played here by local self-governments, persons of authority in local communities, and associations.

Internal Socio-Political Determinants of Reconstruction

Reconstruction is a difficult undertaking, and one that is burdensome to society. It has been carried out at a varying pace by the changing governments, each of which adjusts it to its particular preferences. What does not help this process is the stratification of Polish society, especially the growing number of people living close to, or below, the poverty line. The state budget is unbalanced because of uncollectable taxes, a result of which is the underdevelopment of public services, which in turn is yet another factor bringing down the standard of living (Gilowska, 1993). The cost of living keeps increasing, and food expenses in many families constitute as much as 70–80 per cent of their incomes, pushing aside the satisfaction of such needs as medical care, education for children and leisure. In the case of the poorest families, this leads to drastic reductions in nourishment and even to undernourishment, which causes the already poor health status of society to deteriorate even further (*Sfera społeczna w 1993 roku*, 1994; *Gospodarka Polski w procesie transformacji*, 1994).

The transformation process is not facilitated by the instability of the state's political system, either, or by the aggressive attitude of some trade unions. The wage–price spiral is still at work: successive governments try to compensate for shortages in the wages fund in the budget by pushing up the prices of energy, fuels, transport, alcohol and cigarettes, already much too high in comparison with people's earnings. This is one of the factors keeping inflation invariably at a two-digit level.

External Determinants of Reconstruction

Yet another factor unfavourable for socio-economic transformation is the national debt, which amounted to 46.2 billion US dollars in mid-1994. In this situation the long-term debt reduction (by 50 per cent) negotiated with the Paris Club in 1991, as well as the most recent, 49 per cent reduction of debts by the London Club and its agreement to extend the period of their repayment over many years, can be treated as the support of these institutions for the Polish reforms. The reforms suffer, however, from the poor influx of foreign capital. By mid-1994 foreign investments in Poland totalled 3.5 billion US dollars, which is less than half of the sum of 7.8 billion US dollars declared by the Western countries. The basic reason for this state of affairs is thought to be the imperfection and variability of legal regulations, the uncertainty of the political situation, difficulties with the transfer of capital and the underdevelopment of the technical infrastructure, especially telecommu-nications and the customs clearance procedure. On the other hand, some foreign investors tend to show a purely exploitative attitude towards their Polish ventures, or to invest at a maintenance rather than development level.

The State of the Economy

The Structure of the Economy

The transformation of the economy affects its structure, and changes in the structure may provide a basis for more or less optimistic assessments of the transformation process.

Fundamental changes have been taking place in the structure of the economy: services are gaining prominence while industry and agriculture are losing it. This tendency results not only from the dynamic development of the service sector and structural transformations in industry, but also from a decline in the importance of the latter sector, especially heavy industry, and a crisis in agriculture. In the structure of the economy the private sector has come to the fore: it has dominated trade and services almost completely, and now extends to such formerly state-monopolized domains as finance and foreign trade. The number of private schools, surgeries and clinics also continues to climb.

Industry

The restructuring of industry is both active and passive. On the one hand we witness the collapse of enterprises which are old, inefficient, environmentally unfriendly, employing antiquated technology and unable to market their products for lack of demand, and, on the other hand, many new firms, usually small, are being created. This process is facilitated by the lack of formal or legal restrictions on starting economic activity and the opening of the Polish economy (no barriers to material procurement). These are conditions in which a buyer's (rather than a seller's) market can develop, stimulating the development of flexible manufacturing, attractive and fashionable pattern design, new technologies, and marketing skills. One unsolved problem is the restructuring of the power and fuel industries, which are a serious burden to the economy and society and one cause of the inflationary spiral. It seems that factors in the development and structural transformation of industry might include: government orders; greater domestic demand for consumer goods created by a reversal in the impoverishment tendency; export with no external limitations; and lower interest rates on bank credit.

Agriculture

Agriculture, with its archaic structures unable to adapt to the conditions of a market economy, is in the grip of a deep crisis. The only response of farming to change is to cut down agricultural production and raise the prices of foodstuffs, in a situation whereby the agricultural produce market is artificially protected by a system of countervailing tariffs. Total agricultural production in 1993 was about 40 per cent lower than in 1989. The high prices of agricultural commodities are a major reason for the impoverishment of society, hence for the drop in demand for foodstuffs and other consumer goods, and so are detrimental to the economic development of the country.

International Trade

When the Polish economy functioned within the Comecon and Warsaw Pact system, the character and geographical directions of foreign exchange were clearly defined. When the situation changed in 1989 and it proved difficult to adjust to the new circumstances, an unfavourable balance of trade was recorded in 1991. Data on foreign trade in 1994 seem to indicate that this tendency is gradually being reversed (*Informacja o przebiegu...*, 1994).

Inflation and Unemployment

Inflation is still high, although it has been falling, steadily but too slowly, from 580 per cent in 1990 to 70 per cent in 1991, 47 per cent in 1992 and 35 per cent in 1993. At the time of writing, forecasts for 1994 were not promising; it seems that inflation may far exceed the anticipated level of 27 per cent.

Unemployment, on the rise since 1991, has stabilized at 16 per cent. It is a complex phenomenon, because it comprises three kinds of unemployment: structural, cyclical and frictional.

The State Budget

The state budget falls short of needs it should meet, which is felt most acutely in social services and the budget-dependent sector. Science, education and culture are wrestling with difficulties, the health service and social insurance system are malfunctioning. The material position of the intelligentsia has been deteriorating steadily. More and more people look to social welfare for help. The health status of society is alarmingly bad, mainly owing to its increasing poverty, undernourishment and the crisis in health care services (*Gospodarka Polski w procesie transformacji*, 1994).

Among the main reasons for the budget being so low are: the crisis dragging on in the economy; the effects of privatization being less advantageous than expected; a low level of tax collectability; and misappropriations.

Social Pathologies

The period of transformation favours the spreading of socially pathological behaviour, especially crime. The number of the most serious crimes — homicide, robbery and theft — has been increasing in recent years. Criminals act with growing ruthlessness and cruelty. Organized criminal groups have intensified their activity. Poland has found herself on one of the drug routes of Europe; domestic drug production (amphetamine) is flourishing. The crime detection level is very low (52 per cent). Drug addiction, alcoholism and disguised prostitution are becoming widespread. The number of AIDS carriers, homeless persons and beggars has been growing.

The State of the Environment

The most beneficial changes have occurred in the environment, and its quality has been improving steadily. The level of particulates and gases in the air has diminished, as well as the amount of solid and liquid waste discharged. Also, less water is extracted for economic and municipal purposes. The area of degraded land requiring reclamation has decreased, while the area of woodland has expanded. This is primarily the result of declining industrial production, but also of the restructuring of the economy, especially industry, and the raising of the ecological consciousness of society.

The Economic-Financial Situation of the State

The beneficial effects of the transformation taking place in Poland can be seen in the dynamics of Gross Domestic Product. The year 1992 was the first since 1989 when a positive (2.2 per cent) increment of GDP was recorded. This tendency also prevailed in 1993 (3.8 per cent), which made planners anticipate an increase of 4.5 per cent for the year 1994. Another optimistic sign is a budget deficit lower than expected and a good level of the state's foreign exchange reserves.

It only remains to be hoped that these are steady tendencies indicating that Poland is actually getting over the crisis, and that the changes occurring there are taking the right direction (*Informacja o przebiegu...*, 1994).

Regional Differences in the Period of Socio-Economic Transformation in Poland

During the period of socio-economic transformation, Poland's regional diversification also started to change.

In the beginning, that is, in the late 1980s, there were three classes of regions: strong, average and weak, distinguished by the criterion of their socio-economic development as measured by the GDP generated and distributed in them (see Figure 2.1). Only seven out of the forty-nine regions belonged to the strong class and occupied the highest positions on the scale of regional development. Nineteen regions were classed as weak. Strong regions were urban-industrial centres of the country with prospering agriculture. Weak regions were rural-agricultural in character.

The distribution of these regions showed sharp contrasts: first, at the national scale, between the better developed western part and the retarded eastern part. This division of Poland, determined by historical factors, is deeply ingrained in the country's socio-economic reality. Almost fifty years of post-war Communism and a centrally controlled economy failed to eradicate these 'old' regional disparities. Secondly, at the sub-national scale, between strong regions whose cores are urban-industrial agglomerations and the neighbouring weak regions. These differences, in turn, result from the development strategy of the 1970s based on the conception of polycentric polarization which consisted of forcing the development of large-city regions.

The socio-economic transformation in Poland in the years 1989–93 has varied regionally. It has a different pattern and produces different effects in strong, average and weak regions. It may lead to a change in the status of a region or may fix its character; as a result, it may be conducive to the formation of three alternative models of regional disparities: (1) the equalization of inter-regional differences; (2) a new polarization of the regional system; or (3) the petrification of regional disproportions.

Regional transformation can be considered in terms of particular socio-economic phenomena which are part of this process, and then we have a single-aspect analysis, or in terms of all the phenomena constituting the transformation, which gives a multi-aspectual, synthetic picture of the changing regions.

Main Aspects of the Regional Transformation in Poland

The main components of the socio-economic transformation in Poland which significantly influence regional variations include:

1) changes in industry,
2) changes in the economic structure,
3) privatization of the economy,
4) the inflow of foreign capital,
5) the level of unemployment, and
6) the population's incomes.

We shall use these components to discuss the pattern and effects of regional transformation in a single-aspect approach.

Figure 2.1 Strong, average and weak regions in Poland, 1986

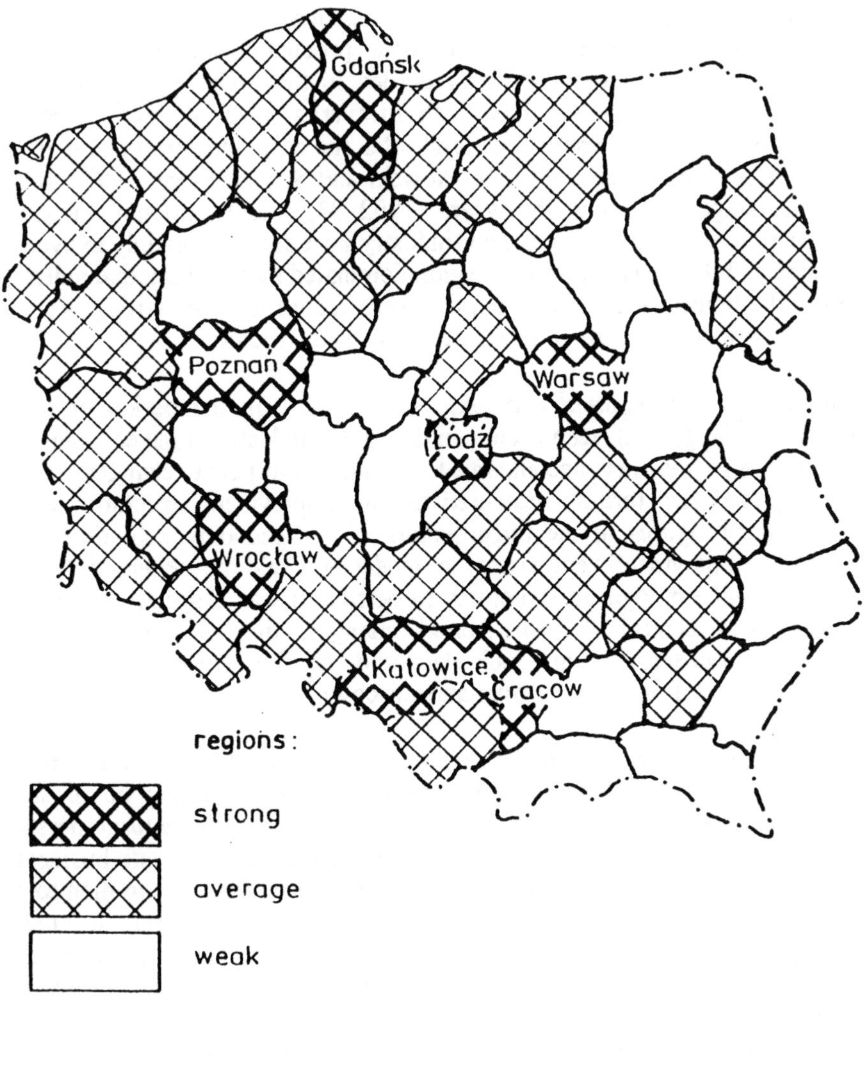

Source: *Dochód narodowy Polski w 1986*, Warsaw, 1989.

Changes in the industrial potential of regions During the first stage of economic transformation in the years 1989–91 the drop in national income (by 18 per cent) was largely the result of a slump in industrial production (by 33 per cent). The decline in industrial production took place in strong regions (the worst recession was recorded in the Łódź region, called the Polish Manchester) and in those with an average level of development, as well as in weak ones, where huge (and often the only) industrial plants of the given regions went bankrupt (Matykowski and Stryjakiewicz, 1992). In the second stage, covering the years 1992–93, when national industrial production increased by 7 per cent, industry kept declining mainly in average regions and the strong Katowice region dominated by the extractive industry, while the highest industrial dynamics were recorded in the strong Warsaw and Cracow regions with a diversified industrial structure.

Changes in the regional economic structures In the period of transformation the general steep decline in the role of industry in the economies of the regions was not accompanied by any significant changes in the intraregional structure as measured by the employment structure. As the employment figures in the three sectors of the economy kept decreasing while unemployment kept rising, a tendency could be observed for the intraregional employment structures to petrify. It was especially distinct in eastern and central Poland. Actual changes, that is, an increase in employment in services, only took place in a very few regions, mainly strong and urbanized (Katowice, Poznań and Cracow).

Privatization of the regional economy In the years 1990–92 the dynamic growth of the private sector was largely due to the setting up of small economic units (employing up to five workers) run by natural persons, especially in trade and services. The distribution of small private businesses over the period in question, whose number increased from 1.1 million to 1.6 million, showed strong spatial concentration: 40 per cent were located in strong regions. The regional distribution of the location quotient as a measure of the saturation of an area with small private firms, mostly service-oriented, reflects not only significant differences between western and eastern Poland in the level of service development, but also in the level of private enterprise.

As a result of privatization of the economy embracing also other types of firms, employment in the private sector outside agriculture increased from 10 per cent of the total in 1989 to 28 per cent in 1992. In the regional pattern, the division into western and eastern regions is even more pronounced here.

The inflow of foreign capital to regions The inflow of foreign capital to Poland, still inadequate to the needs, has taken place through the increase in the number of companies with foreign capital participation. In the years 1990–3 their number climbed from 1,600 to 15,000. Their distribution displays regional regularities in the allocation of the foreign capital. In 1993, strong regions attracted 70 per cent of such companies, with as many as 35 per cent located in the Warsaw region alone (Centralny Urząd Planowania, 1994). The situation was good also in the western frontier regions, but very few companies with foreign capital were located in eastern Poland.

The principal factor attracting foreign investors to particular regions is the level of development of their banking system. In 1993 the greatest number of banks was concentrated in the Warsaw and Poznań regions (15 per cent of the total) and in regions of western and south-western Poland. A deficiency of banks is observed in eastern and central Poland.

The level of regional unemployment In the initial stage of transformation the collapse of the state-run economy in industry and agriculture caused unemployment to appear already at the beginning of 1990. It reached 2.5 million in 1992, and in 1993 climbed to 2.9 million, which meant an unemployment rate of 16 per cent. Two compact areas of high unemployment could be distinguished in the regional structure: that of north-eastern Poland, extending towards central Poland, and a north-western zone (Czyż, 1993). They embrace weak, agricultural regions as well as those with an average level of development and the predominance of either state farms, now being liquidated, or antiquated industry in need of restructuring. Low unemployment levels were recorded mostly in strong regions (with the exception of Łódź), that is, Warsaw, Poznań, Cracow, Katowice and Wrocław. The regional structure of unemployment formed in 1992 and has been very stable since then, which is proof of a prolonged recession in the regions of north-eastern, northern and central Poland, as well as in some western regions.

The regional population's incomes Over the years 1990–92 the order of regions on the scale of earned monthly income changed. Another change was the extent of regional disparities in monthly earnings. There was a marked tendency for wages to fall in regions associated with the extractive industry. The situation improved in regions embracing urban agglomerations and performing multifarious economic functions (for example Warsaw). Invariably the lowest were the incomes of the population in south-eastern Poland. Because of the so-called grey sector of the economy (undeclared incomes), the number of cars per 1,000 population is treated as an additional indicator of people's wealth. In the years 1990–2 this indicator grew from 125 to 169, and its distribution is yet another confirmation of the striking contrast between the advanced western Poland and the lagging east.

The transformation of regions within the particular socio-economic phenomena does not lead to the levelling out of regional differences in Poland, but rather fossilizes them. Socio-economic changes perpetuate the existing disparities between the poorly developed rural-agricultural regions of eastern Poland and the western ones, more advanced, more urbanized and more diversified in their economic structures.

Regional Transformation in a Multi-Aspectual Approach

Regional transformation in a multi-aspectual approach means the occurrence of synthetic socio-economic changes in Poland's regional system. That these changes are significant is proved by the structural evolution accompanying the short process of transformation, detected with the help of principal components analysis.[1]

In the first stage of transformation, in 1990, still under conditions of an economic regression, the main structural dimension of the regional system was the urban-industrial economy. The maintenance of, or shifts in, the positions of the tree types of region (strong, average and weak) on the scale of the urban-industrial economy revealed their resistance to crisis phenomena in the initial period of transformation. By and large, average regions are the ones which have changed their positions by shifting up or down the scale of development. Those of them that have moved up can be called regions with passive resistance to crisis. Their promotion on the scale is associated with the fuel or extractive industries located in them (Płock, Legnica, Tarnobrzeg, Piotrków). Because of the rapid rise in the prices of fuels, energy and raw materials, these regions obtain high values of industrial production sold, in comparison with other regions, even if their production is declining in quantitative terms. Average regions which have fallen down the scale are those with a distinct lack of resistance, dominated by industries responding to crisis with a decline (the electrical equipment and metallurgical industries in the Rzeszów, Kielce, Radom and Lublin regions), or by state-run agriculture now being liquidated (Olsztyn, Słupsk and Koszalin). Also strong regions have differentiated in terms of passive or active resistance to crisis. That the Katowice region has kept its high position on the scale of the urban-industrial dimension despite the breakdown of its economy is evidence of its passive resistance founded on the high economic potential with which it first encountered the recession. The drop in the position of the Łódź region (with its textile industry), in turn, follows from the lack of both passive and active resistance. The

Table 2.1 Poland: classification of regions, 1992

GDP per head (Poland = 100%)	Disposable household incomes (Gross Disposable National Income: GDNI) per head (Poland = 100%)		
	> 100%	100–75%	< 75%
> 100%	WARSAW POZNAŃ CRACOW SZCZECIN LEGNICA ZIELONA GÓRA BYDGOSZCZ GDAŃSK KATOWICE WROCŁAW ŁÓDŹ	Płock Piotrków	
100–75%	Leszno	Bielsko-Biała Jelenia Góra Białystok Olsztyn Tarnów Częstochowa Gorzów Tarnobrzeg Biała Podlaska Koszalin Opole Rzeszów Elbląg Lublin Toruń Chełm Kalisz Piła Konin Radom	
< 75%		Sieradz Ciechanów Wałbrzych Siedlce Krosno Zamość Nowy Sącz Suwałki Słupsk Kielce Włocławek Skierniewice Łomża Ostrołęka Przemyśl	

regions: **STRONG** | **average** | weak

Szczecin = region which has changed class in comparison with 1986.

Source: *Produkt krajowy brutto i dochody ludności wg województw w 1992 r.* (The GDP and the Population's Incomes by Voivodship in 1992), Zakład Badań Statystyczno-Ekonomicznych GUS i PAN, Warsaw, 1994.

remaining strong regions have already displayed active resistance resulting from their diversified economic structure.

In the second stage of transformation, in 1992, already under conditions of slow economic growth, the main structural dimension of the regional system undergoes modification in consequence of the development of the private sector of the economy and an increase in the importance of services. The maintenance of, or shifts in, the position of a region (strong, average or weak) on the scale of the new structural dimension is caused by the cumulation of changes and results in the emergence of new categories of regions: those winning and those losing in the process of transformation. The winning group embraces strong regions. Here the transformation has brought about generally positive results signifying economic development. In each of them, however, the process follows a different trajectory. The winning regions are primarily the active ones: Warsaw and Poznań, which already play the role of the principal growth poles in the country's economy today. A fast pace of favourable economic changes characterizes the Gdańsk region. The Cracow region has clearly reinforced its position in the regional system, while Wroc|aw has clearly weakened its own. The Katowice and Łódź regions are winning regions in a passive way. In the average class only the Legnica, Bielsko-Biała, Bydgoszcz, Szczecin and Zielona Góra regions belong to the winning ones and those in which the transformation runs fairly smoothly, while Kielce and Słupsk are clearly losing regions. Among weak regions marked structural changes stimulating further development can be observed in Konin, Tarnów, Leszno and Kalisz. Most average regions and most weak ones, however, are in a state of economic collapse, and lose.

Regions which win and those which lose in the process of transformation can also be identified by comparing the 1992 classification of regions by the criterion of the relative level of socio-economic development as measured by regional income with the 1986 classification (see Table 2.1 and Figure 2.1).[2] Worth noting is the fact that despite some inter-class shifts treated as symptoms of change of the type of region in terms of the level of development, the 1992 classification replicates the 1986 division.

To sum up, we can state that regional transformation taken as a whole of socio-economic changes has led to a structural modification of the regional system, but has not levelled out regional disparities in Poland.

The Need for a New Regional Policy

The spontaneous course and the results of the transformation of the economy to date indicate that there is a need for activating regional policy in contemporary Poland. Clear symptoms of an economic revival can be observed in strong regions which offer the best conditions for development.

In weak regions the chance of getting out of the recession or stagnation while relying solely on intraregional factors is very slim, largely owing to underdeveloped infrastructure. In this situation the task of the regional policy of the state is to shift from a global to a regional and local perspective, which would help accommodate the differences in economic conditions and the level of social activity in the particular regions. In the years 1990–93 regional policy was characterized by: (1) excessive centralism; (2) uniformity of solutions; (3) scarcity of financial means; (4) failure to fully utilize international investment funds for regional development; and (5) lack of institutions co-ordinating various activities, which contributed to the low effectiveness of the policy. So far regional policy has been designed to cushion the adverse social effects of the process of transformation. The chances to activate this policy increase with the improvement of the macroeconomic condition of the Polish economy and with the acceleration of changes in the territorial organization of the state.

Notes

1 The principal components method was used to reduce twenty characteristics of the regional structure in 1990 and 1992. Component V_1 accounted for 43 per cent of total regional variability in 1990 and differed from component V_1 in 1992, which accounted for 50 per cent of total variability. Use was made of the programme devised by Maćkiewicz and Ratajczak (1993).

2 The 1986 and 1992 estimates of regional income are not comparable because of different calculation methods employed, and hence they do not allow the dynamics of change to be determined. It is only possible to compare the GDP level in regions with the national average in 1986 and 1992 and to estimate the dynamics index of the national GDP (at fixed prices) in the years 1986–92.

References

Centralny Urząd Planowania (1994), *Raport o polityce regionalnej: Diagnoza* (Report on Regional Policy: A Diagnosis), Warsaw.

Chojnicki, Z. (1990), 'The Anatomy of the Crisis of the Polish Economy', in A. Kukliński and B. Jałowiecki (eds), *Local Development in Europe: Experiences and Prospects*, Regional and Local Studies 5, University of Warsaw, Warsaw, pp. 58–87.

Czyż, T. (1993), 'The Regional Structure of Unemployment in Poland', *Geographia Polonica*, 61, pp. 479–96.

Gilowska, Z. (1993), 'Społeczno-polityczne bariery transformacji ustrojowej: Finanse lokalne' (Socio-Political Barriers to the Systemic Transformation: Local Finance), *Transformacja gospodarki*, 42, Instytut Badań nad Gospodarką Rynkową, Lublin.

Gospodarka Polski w procesie transformacji (1993) (Poland's Economy in the Process of Transformation [1993]) (1994), Instytut Rozwoju i Studiów Strategicznych, Warsaw.

Hübner, D. (1992), 'W poszukiwaniu nowego porządku ekonomicznego' (In Search of a New Economic Order), *Ekonomista*, 4, pp. 489–99.

Informacja o przebiegu procesów społeczno-gospodarczych w I półroczu 1994 r. wraz z prognozą do końca 1994 r. (Information about the Progress of Socio-Economic Processes in the First Half-Year of 1994) (1994), Centralny Urząd Planowania, Warsaw.

Krawczyk, R. (1990), *Wielka przemiana: Upadek i odrodzenie polskiej gospodarki* (The Great Transformation: The Fall and Rebirth of the Polish Economy), Oficyna Wydawnicza, Warsaw.

Kubin, J. and Żekoński, Z. (1992), *W poszukiwaniu strategii zmian* (In Search of a Strategy of Change), Centrum Upowszechniania Nauki PAN, Warsaw.

Lewandowski, J. and Szomburg, J. (1990), 'Strategia prywatyzacji' (The Privatization Strategy), *Transformacja gospodarki*, 7, Instytut Badań nad Gospodarką Rynkową, Gdańsk.

Łukawer, E. (1994), 'Niektóre aspekty polityki gospodarczej w okresie transformacji' (Some Aspects of Economic Policy in the Period of Transformation), in S. Lis (ed.), *Transformacja systemu ekonomicznego w Polsce*, Prace Komisji Nauk Ekonomicznych PAN 18, Cracow, pp. 7–26.

Maćkiewicz, A. and Ratajczak, W. (1993), 'Principal Components Analysis', *Computers and Geosciences*, vol. 19, no. 3, pp. 303–42.

Matykowski, R. and Stryjakiewicz, T. (1992), 'The Adaptation of Industry and its Labour Force to the Changing Economic System in Poland', *Erdkunde*, 46, pp. 149–58.

Poland Your Business Partner (1992), Foreign Trade Research Institute, Warsaw.

Poland: The New Business Frontier (1992), Warsaw: Ministry of Foreign Economic Relations.

Sfera społeczna w 1993 roku: Zjawiska i tendencje (The Social Sphere in 1993: Phenomena and Tendencies) (1994), Centralny Urząd Planowania, Warsaw.

Wilczyński, W. et al. (1992), *Drogi wyjścia z polskiego kryzysu gospodarczego* (Ways Out of the Polish Economic Crisis), Akademia Ekonomiczna w Poznaniu, PWN, Warsaw and Poznań.

3 Geographical Aspects of Societal Transformation in the Czech Republic

MARTIN HAMPL and JAN MÜLLER

Introduction

The fundamental societal changes which are taking place after the fall of the totalitarian regime in the Czech Republic are also an important theme for geographical enquiry. First of all, the geographical organization of society is the frame within which transformation processes are carried out and it provides an extremely varied external environment for these processes. Varied conditions result in a varied or uneven course of transformation, not only in the sense of the 'successfulness' of the transformation but also in the sense of its dynamics and direction. The transformation process may be considered from many aspects as a process of geographical diffusion.

Geographical structures must be understood, however, not only as the exogenous conditions under which societal processes take place but also as a specific, integral sub-system of the 'society in its environment'. In this sense, transformation processes necessarily result in changes of geographical organization. Such changes are not as dramatic as changes of economic or political systems, but they are nevertheless major. As an example, we might mention differentiated dynamics in the growth of cities, changes in the regional importance of centres, fundamental changes of the positional attractiveness of centres and their regions and so on. Because of the initial and short-term character of the changes realized so far, we can make only relatively simple observations on the geographical differentiation of the transformation processes. These are predominantly related to the influence of 'traditional' factors of an aggregated type, such as hierarchy of centres and geographical position.

Inversion of the Macropositional Situation and Leading Role of Metropolitan Regions

Basic features or regularities of the regional differentiation of transformation changes may be deduced even from a very simple cartographic assessment of the privatization process, financial sector development, income level of employees and small entrepreneurs or unemployment level. There are major polarizations between west and east, on the one hand, and between metropolitan areas and non-metropolitan areas, on the other. The causes of these polarizations are very simple. Generally we can speak about territorial differentiation in the potential conditions for accepting and developing transformation changes, as a result, on the one hand, of the 'quality' of the population and the range of economic activities in a certain area, and of the accessibility of external sources of development and economic co-operation (simply expressed by the distance from our more developed 'Western' neighbours), on the other. The influence of both types of difference is further fortified by the preceding long-term economic and social development of the Czech space. On the one hand, this has resulted in the elimination of preferences for eastern regions, small (namely district) towns and the heavy industry regions of the socialist era. On the other hand, territorial differences dating from before the Second World War and created during the nineteenth and early twentieth centuries (that is, in the period of classic industrialization and urbanization) have been revived surprisingly quickly. It is only characteristic that this inertia — especially in cultural development — was confirmed by the results of the 1990 elections (see, for example, Jehlicka and Sykora, 1991).

The above characteristics are illustrated by the following assessments of selected empirical phenomena. So as to express the generalized nature of territorial differentiation, a simple method of assessment was used. The Czech Republic was divided into western and eastern parts, on the one hand, and metropolitan and non-metropolitan areas, on the other. The character of the territorial distribution of metropolitan areas enables their even division between the western and eastern halves of the Czech Republic. It is also the case that the population in these areas equals approximately one half of the population of the whole country. Using both aspects, administrative districts (as elementary statistical units) can be divided into four groups with identical population numbers: western metropolitan areas, western non-metropolitan areas, eastern metropolitan areas and eastern non-metropolitan areas. Within the framework of western metropolitan areas, the characteristics of the Prague Metropolitan Area are given so as to stress its exceptional importance.

Selected characteristics of these four parts of the Czech Republic as regards their importance and the level of transformation activity or successfulness in them are presented in Table 3.1. Synthetic assessment is shown in Figure 3.1, which characterizes the unevenness of transformation results by means of the differences in the shares of western and eastern, metropolitan and non-metropolitan parts of the Czech Republic. Twelve 'positive' indicators and one 'negative' indicator (number of unemployed) are included. More detailed information about these characteristics are given in the notes to Table 3.1. In all cases, chosen primarily because of the existence of accessible data, results are similar, that is, above-average occurrence of positive changes or results in the western 'population half' and in the metropolitan 'population half' of the republic. In this sense the importance of the conditional influence of both macroposition and settlement hierarchy is clearly proven. The degree of territorial unevenness assessed, of course, varies according to indicator. The highest is noted in the indicator 'banks' capital' (with Prague in the dominant position), as well as in the number of foreign visitors and the number of joint-ventures. On the other hand, the territorial distribution of the number of entrepreneurs is almost even.

Graphical representation of the chosen indicators demonstrates the combined influence of macropositional and hierarchical factors and their almost even significance (influence of the polarization between metropolitan and non-metropolitan is slightly more important). If we rank these areas of the Czech Republic according to their transformation successfulness we get the following: western metropolitan areas first, followed by eastern metropolitan areas, then slightly further behind are western non-metropolitan areas and finally, much further behind, non-metropolitan areas. In the first group, the highest ranking — Prague and its metropolitan area — should be distinguished because this territorial unit shows the highest degree of 'successfulness'. But even if we eliminate this unit from the assessment, the ranking of the Czech Republic's four parts quoted above remains unchanged. As a conclusion, we can point out not only the prominent importance of principal geographical factors on differentiation in the transformation processes, but also the complex nature of the transformation process and the correspondent high territorial differentiation between indicators of partial changes.

Secondary Features of Territorial Differentiation in the Transformation Processes

The preceding examination results in clear conclusions as to the differentiating importance of basic geographical factors. Certainly this can also be explained by the generalizing nature of the chosen method of assessment. At a more detailed or more sensitive level of study, 'regularities' are not so obvious and on the contrary the influence of specific factors on variability increases. This corresponds to the nature of geographical reality, where we find clear regularities only in basic differentiation, while the secondarily important, individual variabilities of partial territorial units are masked (see also Hampl, 1994). In this chapter we cannot assess territorial differentiation in the transformation processes in the Czech Republic at a more specifically local level. We can, however, try to establish some further differentiating factors which show the possibility of characterizing individual peculiarities. This individualization can be illustrated (though on the level of the districts only) by Figure 3.2, showing the degree of unemployment and the relative level of inciomes of municipalities and districts according to income taxes from employees and small entrepreneurs (an indirect characteristic of incomes level with the proviso that districts with higher in-commuting are at an advantage).

Though cartograms show the two basic types of polarization mentioned — 'west–east' (especially in the case of unemployment) and 'metropolitan–non-metropolitan areas' (especially in the case of income taxes) — we can find many irregularities. It is obvious that the four delimited categories of districts are not internally homogenous. Even in the case of the metropolitan districts, which are limited in numbers, differences are significant. The most important of them, that is, the Prague Metropolitan Area, has already been mentioned. Other specific cases are districts in two main coal-mining areas: the Úst' nad Labem-Most region and the Ostrava region. These show generally less favourable characteristics (see also the level of unemployment) resulting from a high incidence of heavy industry, limited diversification of economic activities and ecological problems (both environmental and social).

Individual differences between districts within the framework of the non-metropolitan areas are of course even more complex. These are the result, on the one hand, of the above-mentioned macropositional differentiation 'west–east', and, on the other, of differentiation in settlement intensity, in the share of agriculture and in economic diversification (which also varies from north to south). In the specific case of Bohemia this results in some equalization between the positional (meaning 'exogenous') advantages of territories along the Bavarian and Austrian borders and the 'endogenous' advantages of northern areas. In the initial phases of transformation, exogenous factors

Table 3.1 Selected characteristics of geographical differentiation of transformation changes in the Czech Republic

Indicators	Categories of districts: % share of the Czech Republic			
	Metropolitan		Non-metropolitan	
	Western (of which Prague Metropolitan)	Eastern	Western	Eastern
A. Basic indicators				
Population	25 (13)	25	25	25
Population increase 1961–91	25 (10)	55	5	15
Area	11 (2)	13	44	32
Jobs in primary sector	10 (4)	18	36	36
Jobs in tertiary sector	34 (22)	25	21	20
University graduates	39 (29)	28	16	17
Population with full secondary level education	29 (18)	25	24	22
B. Characteristics of transformation process				
1. Capital of the banks	88 (82)	8	3	1
2. Income taxes from employees	39 (26)	26	19	16
3. Income taxes from small entrepreneurs	43 (31)	22	19	16
4. Goods production in industry	31 (16)	29	23	17
5. Financial value of small privatization	38 (19)	20	23	19
6. Number of entrepreneurs	31 (20)	22	24	23
7. Number of joint-stock companies	48 (39)	21	16	15
8. Number of joint ventures	55 (40)	23	14	8
9. Number of jobs in joint ventures	43 (30)	17	30	10
10. Number of foreign visitors in accommodation facilities	59 (46)	13	17	11
11. Net migration 1991–93	67 (61)	22	5	6
12. Job vacancies	41 (27)	16	28	15
13. Unemployed	11 (2)	30	24	35

Notes to Table 3.1 overleaf

Notes

The Czech Republic was divided by means of the districts as elements into 4 parts equal as to their population size. The western 'half' is composed of districts in the former provinces of Bohemia excluding Eastern Bohemia Province but including one of the Eastern Bohemia districts (Semily). The following districs in the western part were labelled 'metropolitan': Praha, Praha-vychod, Praha-západ (these form the Prague Metropolitan Area), České Budójovice, Plzeń-město, Sokolov, Karlovy Vary, Most, Teplice, Ústí nad Labem, Liberec, Jablonec nad Nisou. In the Eastern part the 'metropolitan' districts were: Hradec Králové, Pardubice, Brno- město, Brno-venkov, Prostójov, Olomouc, Zlín, Opava, Novy Jičín, Ostrava- město, Karviná, Frydek-Místek.

Sources

Characteristics of the A group are from the Population Censuses of 1991 and 1961. Characteristics of the B group are from the following sources:

1. *Lidové noviny*, 16 March 1994 (data as of 1 March 1994).

2, 3. Internal material from the Ministry of Finance of the Czech Republic, data for January–September 1993.

4, 5, 10. *Statistické informace*, 22 — regionální statistika za r. 1992, ČSÚ, Prague.

6, 8, 9. Internal material from ČSÚ; data as of 31 December 1993, in the case of the number of jobs in joint ventures, these are partly based on estimation

7, 12. Statistické informace, 22 — regionální statistika za 1. pololetí 1993, ČSÚ, Prague, data as of 30 June 1993

11. *Pohyby obyvatelstva v české republice 1991–1993*, ČSÚ, Prague.

13. Aktuality ČSÚ 1993, srpen, ČSÚ, Prague; data as of 31 August 1993.

which support a rapid development of forms of economic activity not overly dependent on capital (such as services connected with tourism for foreign visitors) seem to be more important. From a longer-term perspective it is justifiable to assume that local conditions — the economic and social quality of the population, industrial efficiency and so on — will have a greater influence. Teritorial differentiation in local and regional conditions of this type will in many respects emerge only gradually, due in part to the protracted nature of the main transformation process (the so-called great privatization). In this sense we can also expect further territorial differentiation in the social and economic spheres and an erosion of regularities in the spatial forms of this differentiation, resulting from a greater complexity of the conditions giving rise to it.

The Problem of Territorial Development Proportionality: Concluding Remarks

The present transformation process clearly shows the increased role of selective tendencies, which deepen differentiation at the level of geographical as well as social structures. It is probable at the same time that these tendencies will become yet more dominant in the near future. This is undoubtedly connected with the principal characteristic of the transformation, i.e. the fundamental changes in societal organization, but also with the particularly dramatic nature of change in the initial period of transformation. In later periods we can expect the development of different 'compensation' processes as a result of increasing ecological and technical barriers to growth in most 'exposed' metropolitan areas, and also as a result of social and regional politics which help weak units in order to establish social stability in the whole national system. The relative unevenness of territorial development will always be preserved, however, and the attempts to justify this unevenness and discussion of how to restrict its social consequences will always continue.

There are several causes for this situation, but two of them are specifically geographical. The first is the nature of physio-geographical reality, which creates uneven conditions for societal development — for example the distribution of natural resources or more generally of favourable natural conditions. The secondary, but gradually more and more dominant cause, is the way society actively adapts to external conditions, an adaptation intensified by the principles of effective territorial division of labour — see primarily the advantages contributed by concentration of population, capital and information. In both cases we believe that these causes are objectively given and that it is not only unnecessary but even harmful to ideologize them or to re-evaluate them from an ethical point of view. In this sense, we refute as untrue the various Marxist conceptions of well-proportioned or even development, as well as the exclusive assignment of non-proportioned or uneven development to the capitalist system only (see, for example, Smith, 1990). It is of course beyond doubt that industrialization and urbanization processes connected primarily with the beginning and development of capitalism led to the dynamization of differentiation processes. They also led, however, to the dynamization of societal development as a whole! Such development is inconceivable without differentiation as a source of change and without flexibility to facilitate change and adaptation. It seems that 'unevenness' should be analyzed more profoundly, because its role in the development of society (and indeed in development in the natural world) is irreplaceable. We should reflect on how to put geographical unevenness to effective use and how to create suitable self-regulating mechanisms for finding an appropriate degree of unevenness in the development of society.

References

Blažek, J. (1994), 'Changing Local Finances in the Czech Republic Half Way Over?', *GeoJournal*, vol. 32, no. 3, pp. 261–7.

Dostál, P. and Hampl, M. (1994), 'Development of an Urban System: General Conception and Specific Features in the Czech Republic', in M. Barlow, P. Dostál and M. Hampl (eds), *Territory, Society and Administration: The Czech Republic and Industrial Region of Liberec*, University of Amsterdam, Amsterdam.

Hampl, M. (1994), 'Environment, Society and Geographical Organization: The Problem of Integral Knowledge', *GeoJournal*, vol. 32, no. 3, pp. 191–8.

Jehlička, P. and Sykora, L. (1991), 'Stabilita regionální podpory tradičních politickych stran v českych zemích (1920–1990) (The stability of regional suffrage for traditional parties in the Czech lands [1920–1990]), *Sborník české geografické společnosti*, vol. 96, no. 2, pp. 81–95.

Musil, J. (1992), 'Czechoslovakia in the Middle of Transition', *Czechoslovak Sociological Review*, Special Issue, vol. 28, pp. 5–21.

Smith, N. (1990), *Uneven Development: Nature, Capital and the Production of Space*, 2nd edn., Oxford.

Figure 3.1 Basic characteristics of geographical differentiation of transformation changes in the Czech Republic

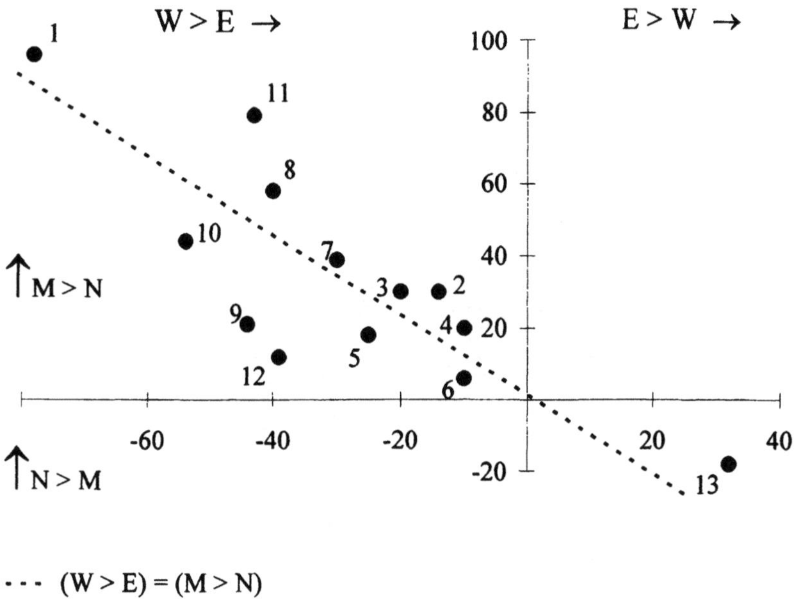

Notes

Basic characteristics of the geographical differentiation of transformation changes
W = Western part of the Czech Republic
E = Eastern part of the Czech Republic
M = metropolitan areas
N = non-metropolitan areas
1–12 = indicators of positive transformation changes (see Table 1)
13 = unemployment

The position of the indicators is determined by the differences between the shares of the western and eastern parts of the Czech Republic and at the same time by the differences between the shares of the metropolitan and non-metropolitan areas. The occurrence of all 'positive' characteristics on the left upper quadrant corresponds to the above-average concentration of the given phenomena when compared to the distribution of population both in the Western and metropolitan parts of the Czech Republic. The dotted axis, (W > E) = (M > N), represents the equivalence between the macropositional and hierarchical differentiation. For more detailed explanation see notes to Table 3.1 and the text.

Figure 3.2 Regional pattern of unemployment in the Czech Republic (31 August 1993)

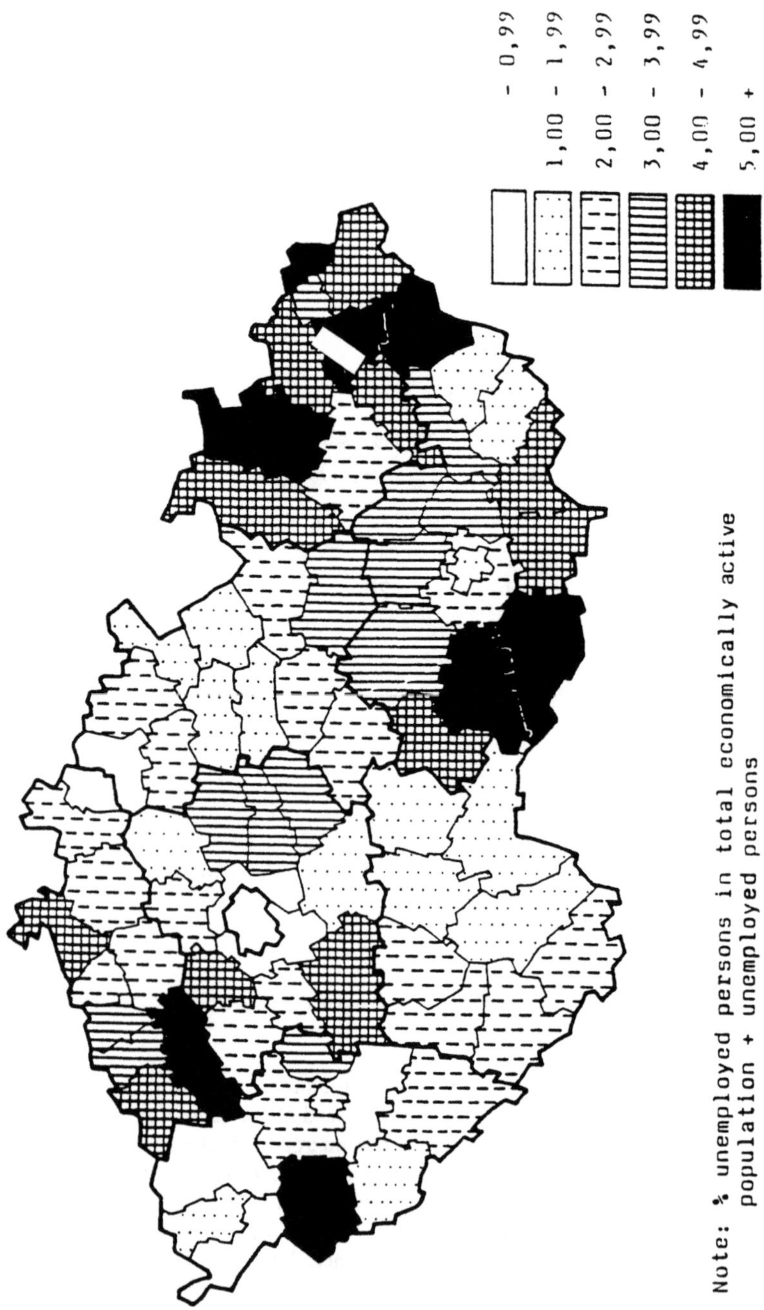

Note: % unemployed persons in total economically active population + unemployed persons

Figure 3.3 Income tax from employees and small entrepreneurs (in Czech crowns, per capita, January–September 1993)

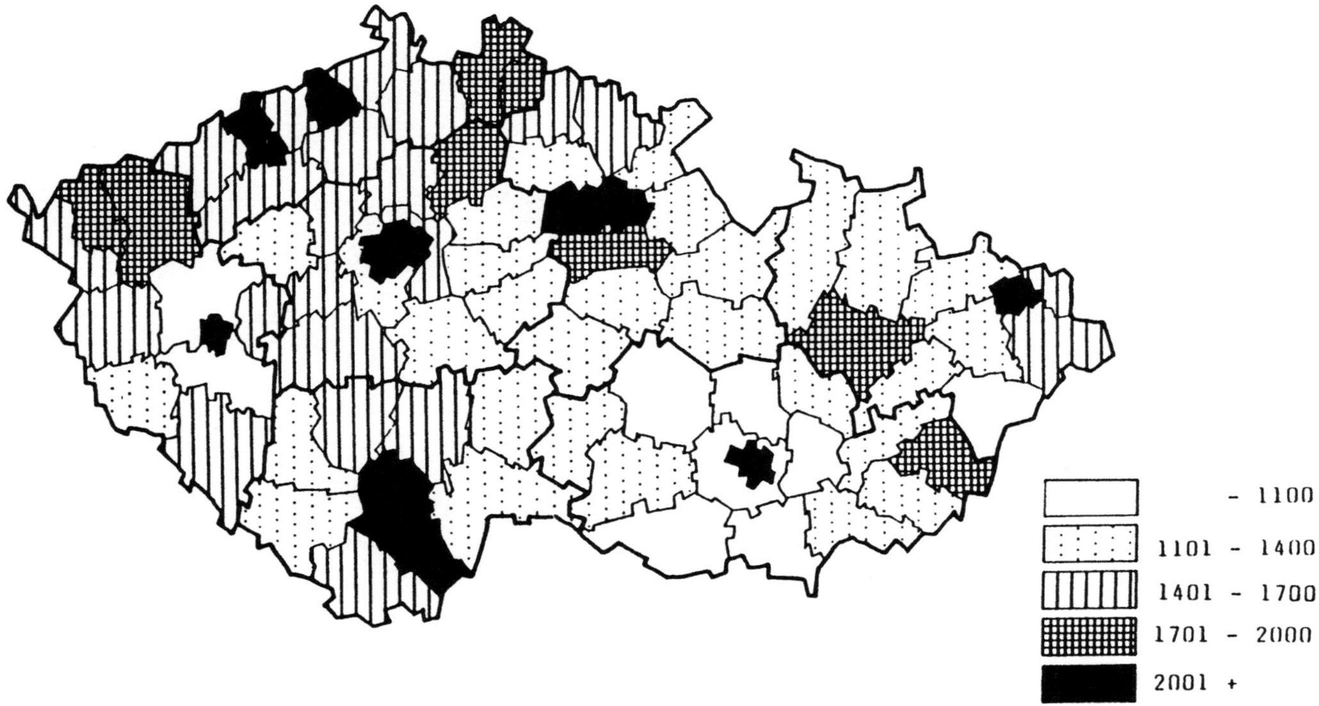

4 Some Features and Problems of the Transformation Process in Slovakia

JÁN PAULOV

Introduction

The transformation process, which aims to transform centrally planned or command economies into economies based on market mechanisms, has both general and specific features. In the case of Slovakia, a specific feature is the intersection of transformation with the construction of a new state, which makes the whole process more complex. The transformation process, which started in Slovakia in 1990 (before the break-up of Czecho-Slovakia), was based upon 'shock therapy' — rapid privatization, a much-hoped-for rapid inflow of foreign capital, the liberalization of prices and foreign trade, and restrictive monetary, budgetary and wage policies with the aim of blocking inflationary pressures and the closure of inefficient enterprises. 'Shock therapy' has been continued in both of the successor states after the break-up of Czecho-Slovakia. After nearly five years of transformation we are in a position to begin to assess its impacts. I have divided this period into two sub-periods: 1990–92 and 1993 onwards, after Slovak independence.

The Transformation Process in the First Period

Table 4.1 provides some macroeconomic indicators for the first three years of transformation. The worst year in terms of economic performance was clearly 1991. There was some slight improvement in 1992 even though shock therapy policies continued to be implemented. But economic decline was occurring within the context of the loss of former COMECON markets while Western markets were largely inaccessible either because of the limited competitiveness of Slovak products or because of Western protectionism. There was, however, an additional factor specific to the Slovak context — the conversion of the armaments industry. In 1988 Slovak military production accounted for 65 per cent of Czechoslovak military output (Schmögnerová, 1993). Decisions by the Czecho-Slovak government to stop armaments production, however, meant that the Slovak economy was hit hardest. The stoppage of armaments production led to both the loss of state revenue and the loss of a relatively stable market, and contributed to the growth of unemployment. Armaments conversion continues to be a major burden on the Slovak state.

The Slovak economy also had to face a problem that continues today — the restructuring of the sectoral structure of the economy. Slovakia has a relatively large share of industries at the lower end of processing along with industries which demand high energy and material inputs. For instance, in 1992 the mining and energy sectors, and the metal and metal goods sectors represented 14.5 per cent and 13.8 per cent of production, respectively.

Table 4.1 Slovakia: selected macro-economic indicators

Indicator	1990	1991	1992
Gross domestic product (% change)	-2.5	-15.8	-6.8
Consumer prices (% change)	10.4	61.2	10.0
Real industrial wages (% change)	-6.6	-27.6	6.8
Unemployment rate (%)	1.5	11.8	10.4
Industrial production (% change)	-3.4	-10.6	-10.6
Agricultural production (% change)	-7.2	-7.4	-11.9

Source: *Hospodárske noviny*, 2 June 1993

Furthermore, if we develop the theory of production chains from Western economic literature (Dicken, 1994), it is clear that the Slovak economy has a large element of low value-added production. As Dicken (1994) has argued, a fundamental problem in integration into the global economy continues to be a country's position in value-added production chains.

The Transformation Process in the Second Period

This period focuses on the break-up of Czecho-Slovakia and the rise of the new successor states. Indeed, the intersection of the transformation with the need to build a new state has made the whole process more complex. Nineteen ninety-three saw further economic decline in Slovakia. For example, against 1992 levels, GDP declined by 4.1 per cent, industrial production by 13.5 per cent, output in the construction sector by 26.1 per cent, and the value of transported goods dropped by 31.4 per cent (Okáli et al., 1994, p. 176). Only in the retailing and the repair, restaurant and accommodation sectors was there an increase of 10.1 per cent. Thus only the service sector was not prone to decline and consequently was able partially to compensate for losses elsewhere in the economy. Unemployment increased to 12.5 per cent in the first half of 1993 and to 14.4 per cent in the second half of the same year (*Monitor of the Economy of the Slovak Republic*, 1994, part I: see Figures 4.1 and 4.2).

The major cause for this decline was the inability to continue the operation of many economic relations and processes arising from the disintegration of the Czecho-Slovak economy. Other factors affected economic performance in 1993, however The separation of currencies, tax reform, and recession in Western market economies all had a negative influence on output in the Slovak economy. However, the development of positive relations between the Czech and Slovak economies was seen in the agreement to establish a customs union and clearing accounts.[1]

A 10 per cent devaluation of the Slovak *koruna* (Sk) occurred in 1993 as a result of these economic problems, which were added to by a high budget deficit (23 billion Sk) and falling labour productivity. Patterns of investment showed a decline larger than GDP change, although the change was uneven between branches of the economy.

During 1994 there was a slight improvement in the economic situation. Data presented in Table 4.2 indicate the dimensions of this turnaround. Other indicators also demonstrate this change. For example, there was an increase in stock held in convertible currencies. Clearly the economic improvement is not great but it does appear, as Slovak economists now argue, that the negative effects of the break-up are beginning to be overcome.

Table 4.2 Slovakia: basic indicators of national economic development

Indicator	1993 2nd quarter	1993 3rd quarter	1993 4th quarter	1994 1st quarter	1994 2nd quarter
Inflation (% change)	20.7	22.4	23.2	15.5	14.6
Cost of living index	120.6	122.1	122.2	115.4	114.7
Unemployment (%)	12.5	13.7	14.4	14.5	14.1
Balance of the state budget (million Sk)	-14,822	-15,899	-23,011	-5,955	-10,512

Source: *Monitor of the Economy of the Slovak Republic*, 1994, Part I.

Figure 4.1 Slovakia: unemployment rate (%) in the former large administrative units (December 1990–February 1994)

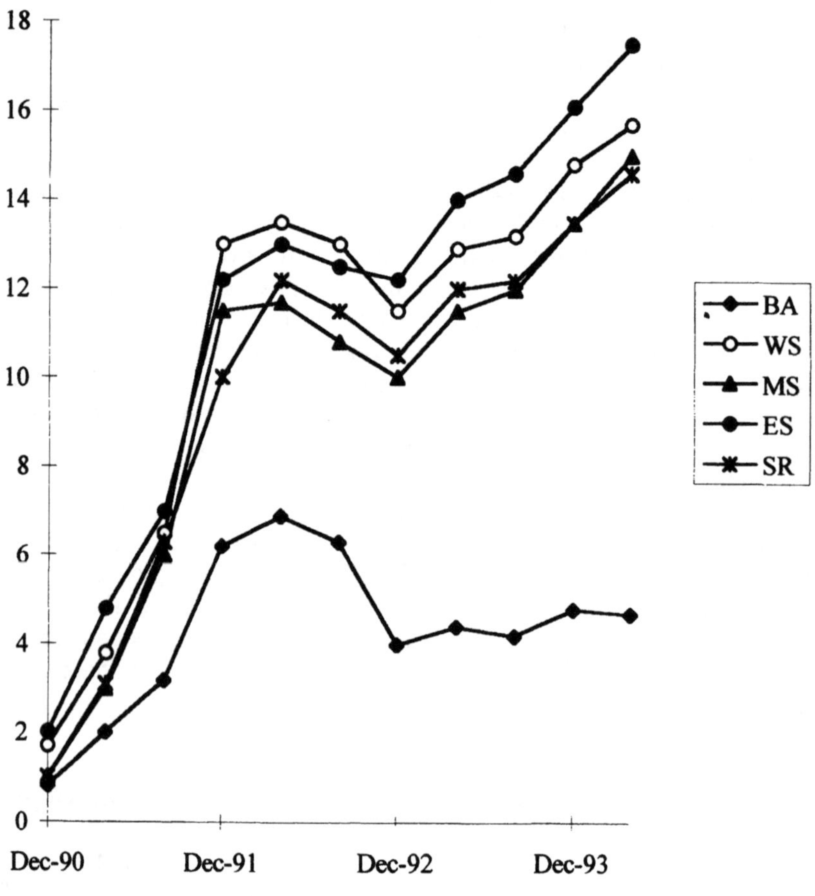

BA = Bratislava; WS = West Slovak region; MS = Middle Slovak region; ES = East Slovak region; SR = Slovak Republic

Source: Rajcáková, 1994.

Figure 4.2 Slovakia: unemployment rate, 31 January 1993

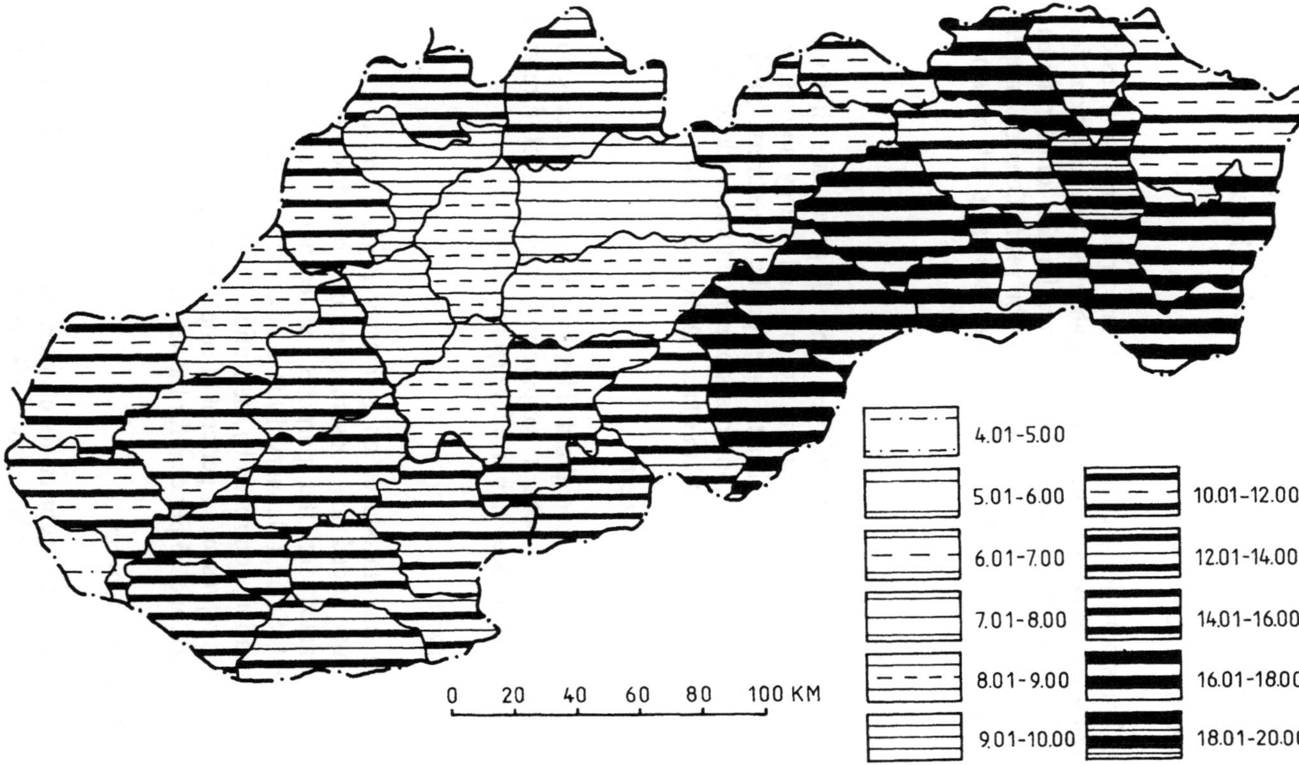

The Transformation Process: A Partial Summary

The transformation process between 1990 and the first half of 1994 appears, therefore, to be characterized by the following elements:

Property rights

The Transformation Act provided the basic rules for the transformation of state-owned property. Further laws established the conditions for property transformation in the co-operative sector, for the transformation of state-ownership into commercial ownership, for restrictions on property claims between 1948 and 1989, and for the ownership of housing and non-residential space.

Price liberalization

Currently, approximately 95 per cent of prices are liberalized. Price regulation remains, however, in the fuel and energy sectors, water, mail, telecommunications, rent, health care, public investment, public transport and state guaranteed price purchases of agricultural products. It is likely that prices will be liberalized in these areas in the near future.

Foreign trade liberalization

Foreign trade is fully liberalized. There is an average customs duty of 5 per cent, and there has been a temporary introduction of foreign exchange payment restrictions to stabilize foreign reserves.

Taxation reform

Tax reform was introduced on 1 January 1993. There are eight types of taxation (value added tax, consumption tax, profit tax, etc.). Tax holidays can be granted for the purposes of economic and regional policy development. Since 1 January 1993 a new social security system has also been in operation, controlled by the National Insurance Company. Insurance contributions represent 11 per cent of employee wages, a level of 35 per cent for employers, and 16 per cent for the self-employed.

Social security network

A minimum wage, subject to changes in the cost of living, has been implemented, which in November 1993 was set at 2,450 Sk. While wages in

1993 were not subject to regulation, they have been since 1994. Those people with incomes below the minimum wage can apply for assistance. Unemployment benefit is paid for six months: 55 per cent of the previous wage for the first three months, falling to 50 per cent for the following three months. During re-qualification benefits are paid up to 75 per cent of the previous wage. Pensions are adjusted according to the cost of living, and have already been changed three times.

The establishment of new financial institutions

Following the establishment of the National Bank of Slovakia (NBS) the banking sector has evolved rapidly. At the end of 1993 there were seventeen domestic banks, nine subsidiaries of foreign banks, and seven bank-affiliated companies. Since 1994, however, more rigorous financial conditions (500 million Sk as basic capital) have been set for the establishment of new banks. The capital market functions through the Bratislava stock exchange. The Bratislava Option Exchange and the RMS Slovakia company all trade in shares from the voucher privatization programme.

Restructuring and privatization in the enterprise sector

'Small privatization' of shops, services and small enterprises is virtually complete. Some 9,676 privatized entities have been created and revenue from privatization amounted to 14.5 billion Sk. The first wave of the 'large privatization' was completed in 1993. The second wave was somewhat delayed during 1994, but it has now begun again.

The Transformation Process: Some Notes on the Re-Privatization of Agriculture

The privatization of the agricultural sector demands special attention, although a detailed treatment is beyond the scope of this paper. Privatization is occurring. Up to February 1994, for example, 123,784 people made claims on 179,961 hectares of land. Of these, 99,639 cases were successfully concluded with the return of 143,115 hectares. However, about 81,000 cases involve the return of only two hectares of land or less. Only 154 people have requested the return of more than 50 hectares (*Statistical Report...*, 1994). Consequently, the privatization of land over 50 hectares has been quite slow. This is largely because agricultural production costs are high, requiring significant levels of investment. As a result, small farmers with below two hectares of land tend to produce fruit and vegetables for domestic consumption or for small-scale commercial production. They can therefore not be regarded as fully-fledged farmers.

Agricultural co-operatives under the Communist system did, however, operate quite effectively. They also tended to be technically well equipped, and to have highly educated management personnel. Incomes of co-operative members were often high and living standards were good, with many owning their own family housing. Therefore, it remains an open question as to whether it is optimal to transform co-operative farms into a private agricultural sector. What is probably necessary is the reduction of the size of the labour attached to co-operatives along with increases in efficiency. However, this is a difficult period to undertake agricultural restructuring because farm subsidies have been dramatically reduced, while they still remain high in Western economies. Consequently, agricultural unemployment tends to be high.

The Transformation Process: Some Notes on Spatial Patterns and Regional Policy

Few clear spatial patterns or regularities are evident, although there do seem to be emerging a series of development gradients between (a) urban and rural areas, (b) industrial and agricultural localities, (c) core and peripheral regions (inland–borderland differences), and (iv) areas located in the west and those in the east. In addition there are two large metropolitan areas in which specific processes are operating — Bratislava and Košice — and where transformation has occurred far more rapidly than elsewhere. By combining and overlaying these elements we can gain a better understanding of the dimensions of regional differentiation.

In terms of policy development, one of the basic priorities should be the re-evaluation of the geographical position of Slovakia. Slovakia could benefit from the eradication of east–west barriers in Europe by acting as a central European transit country between east and west, and north and south, although it is necessary to build a modern transportation infrastructure. Furthermore, the enhancement of cross-border relations with Austria and Hungary could be strengthened in the creation of a Euroregion. This border region has excellent potential as it contains the second largest river in Europe, the Danube. With the completion of the Danube–Main–Rhine canal the Danube can operate as a force for integration in Europe with the river region comprising two metropolitan cores, Vienna in Austria and Bratislava in Slovakia separated by only 65 km. The existence of historical ties through the Austro-Hungarian empire suggests that preconditions for such cross-border developments are already present.

Note

1 The customs union is no longer valid. The Czech Republic reneged on the agreement on clearing accounts in 1995.

References

Dicken, P. (1994), 'Global–Local Tensions: Firms and States in the Global Space-Economy', *Economic Geography*, vol. 7, no. 2, pp. 101–28.

Monitor of the Economy of the Slovak Republic, 1994, vol. 6, part 1.

Okáli, I. et al. (1994), 'Economic Development of the Slovak Republic in 1993', *Ekonomický časopis*, vol. 42 no. 3, pp. 174–206.

Rajčáková, E. (1994), 'The Main Character of Process and State of Unemployment in Slovakia', *Acta Facultatis Rerum Naturalium Universitatis Comenianae, Geographica*, no. 34, pp. 173–89.

Schmögnerová, B. (1993), 'Konverzia v podnikoch Slovenskej republiky v transformačnom období' (The conversion of enterprises in Slovakia during the transformation), *Ekonomický časopis*, vol. 41 no. 4, pp. 253–70.

'Správa o Slovensku' (Report on Slovakia), *Hospodárske noviny*, 2 June 1993.

Štatistická správa o základných vývojových tendenciách v národnom hospodárstve SR v 1. štvrťroku 1994 a ich predikcii na rok 1994 (Statistical Report on Economic Developments in Slovakia for the First Quarter of 1994 and Predictions for 1994), Štatistický úrad Slovenskej republiky (Slovak Statistical Office).

5 Recent Changes in the Socio-Economic Structure of Slovenia

MARIJAN M. KLEMENČIĆ

Introduction

The Republic of Slovenia, although small in size, is extremely diverse. The four most important natural geographic regions of Europe intersect within the 20,256 square kilometres of Slovenian territory: the Alps, the Pannonian plain, the Dinaric mountain range and the Mediterranean Sea.

For centuries Slovenia was part of the Habsburg Empire. It was within this framework of Central Europe that it underwent the first phase of industrialization. Later political developments — the inclusion of Slovenia in Yugoslavia — gave emphasis to the cultural, economic and political influence of the Balkans, but the centuries-long ties with Central Europe were never completely severed.

Especially after the Second World War Slovenia experienced massive changes in its social and economic structure. In the 1950s half the active population was employed in agriculture, while in 1991 this figure was 13 per cent. In 1990 Slovenia achieved GNP per capita of roughly 5,000 US dollars.

The 1990s represent a critical turning-point for Slovenia, as for many other European countries. The first democratic elections of the post-war period took place in April 1990, while in December of the same year the population decided in favour of independence by an overwhelming majority (90 per cent) in a referendum. In June 1991, after successfully rebuffing an attack by the former Yugoslav army, Slovenia affirmed its existence as an independent state.

The purpose of this chapter is to present the most important socio-economic and spatial changes undergone by Slovenia during the transition from a socialist to a market economy and as an independent nation. It rests on a brief outline of earlier development, concentrating on those areas deemed crucial for an understanding of the present socio-economic and spatial structure of Slovenia: demographic development, economic structure, socio-economic development, unemployment, ethnic structure of the population and urbanization.

We start from the hypothesis that the social, political and economic changes of the 1990s do not represent an entirely new era but rather a rapid acceleration of processes which already indicated the gradual movement of Slovenia towards a market economy and political democracy. The following factors have had an influence on this:

- The geographic location of Slovenia as a neighbour of Austria and Italy has encouraged its adaptation to demanding Western markets.
- The varied relief and diverse regional structure of the country foster polycentric economic development and small- and medium-sized companies and industries.
- Important transportation routes which intersect in Slovenia enhance its ties with other countries.
- The small size of the domestic market and a relatively well-developed economy stimulate a trade- and export-oriented economy.
- The socialist system was mitigated by the systemic variant of self-management, which enabled a higher level of economic and social innovation and initiative than did central planning.
- A high degree of autonomy granted to its constituent republics by Yugoslavia meant that Slovenia was free to develop its potential unfettered.

Demographic Potential

During the post-war period the population increased from 1,466,000 in 1953 to 1,966,000 in 1991. Until the end of the Second World War there was an intensive emigration by the Slovene population to Western European countries, the USA, Canada, Argentina and Australia. The demographic structure of Slovenia was therefore doubly affected: by constant emigration and wartime casualties. Slovenia lost its younger generations to foreign lands.

In the post-war period Slovenia experienced the concluding phase of this demographic transition. The highest fertility rate was achieved in 1950 (2.4 per cent), the lowest in 1992 (1.0 per cent). The death rate hovered at around 1.0 per cent throughout the post-war period, such that Slovenia has moved from zero to negative population growth.

This unfavourable natural growth rate of the population was accompanied by similarly unfavourable post-war migration trends. In 1980 the migration balance was 2.8, in 1990 it was 1.1, and was negative by the following year (-1.5). The cause of this development is more than apparent: a drop in immigration from the republics of the former Yugoslavia due to the political independence of Slovenia and the introduction of legislation aimed at regulating the inflow of foreigners.

Development of the Slovene Economy

The economic structure of Slovenia reflects the imprints of two distinct periods: Austro-Hungarian and Yugoslav. In both cases the Slovene economy was just part of a larger economic system.

The first period, the Austro-Hungarian, was characterized by the beginning of industrialization and the development of transport infrastructure, especially railways, from the north towards the Adriatic Sea (Trieste). The Slovene economy was marginal within the context of the Habsburg state and limited mainly to the exploitation and processing of local resources such as coal, timber, mercury and other natural resources, and to the beginnings of industrial sectors producing goods for mass consumption, such as textiles, footwear and food products. An important factor in the development of industry was the tradition of the labour force, which in numerous regions already had experience of domestic crafts (manufacturing of wooden articles, shoemaking, pottery and so on), which made possible the survival of the peasant population on small farms and in many places meant the beginning of industrial production. In 1910 about 11 per cent of the active population was employed in industry.

The Yugoslav period occurred as two different periods (the inter-war and the post-war/socialist), which none the less had common features. The Slovene economy, as the most developed in the new state, was completely reoriented towards the Yugoslav market. Tariffs protected the economy against external shocks. In the inter-war period, with the opening of the Yugoslav market, industry expanded greatly (textiles, metalworking, metallurgy and coal-mining). In 1939, 20 per cent of the active population was employed in industry. After the Second World War industry developed even more rapidly. In 1989 the most important sectors were metalworking and machine-building (23 per cent of the workforce), textiles (15 per cent), electronics and electrical goods (14 per cent), wood-working and furniture-making (6 per cent) and chemicals (6 per cent).

The 1990s represent a third turning point in the development of the Slovene economy over the last hundred years. With some qualification it could be said that Slovenia is returning to the Central European capitalist economic space. And this time, too, as in the past, Slovenia is acting as a marginal, economically less developed part of Europe.

Table 5.1 Regional structure of Slovenian imports in 1992 (%)

European Community	45.8
Germany	18.1
EFTA	11.8
Austria	8.5
Other industrialized countries	6.0
Developing countries	4.1
Other countries	10.8
Former Yugoslav republics	21.6
Total	100.0

Table 5.2 Regional structure of Slovenian exports in 1991 and 1992 (%)

	1991	1992
European Community	31.5	50.2
EFTA	4.0	6.9
Other industrialized countries	3.0	4.9
Developing countries	2.0	4.2
Other countries	6.1	8.3
Former Yugoslav republics	53.3	25.5
Total	100.0	100.0

Source: Statistical Yearbook of the Republic of Slovenia, 1993.

Such major changes have a strong influence on the whole regional structure, including the transport and energy infrastructure, settlement, land use and so on. The major transportation axes have changed three times in the last century: first, they ran predominantly from north to south (Vienna–Trieste) before the First World War, then from north-west to south-east (Western Europe to the Near and Middle East) under Yugoslavia, and finally from south-west to north-east (from the Adriatic Sea and northern Italy to Central and Eastern Europe) in the 1990s and beyond.

Despite strong concentrations of industry and population, typical of an industrial economy, the policy of regional development with an emphasis on industry contributed significantly to the development of rural areas. Especially in the 1970s a number of small industrial plants were established in rural and underdeveloped areas. Thus there are 464 settlements in Slovenia with some industry: of these, 335 have fewer than 500 people employed in industry and only ten towns have more than 5,000 employed in industry.

Post-war Social and Economic Development

The economic development of Slovenia was strongly based on industrialization. The basic weakness of industry lay in the very slow pace of its modernization and restructuring. Up until the 1980s Slovenia industrialized very intensively: not until the 1990s was there an observable decline in the importance of industry relative to tertiary activities.

Table 5.3 Slovenia: number of workers employed in industry and their share of the active population

Year	1953	1961	1971	1981	1991
Number	119,969	192,423	270,410	328,522	314,033
%	14.5	25.0	32.3	38.1	35.7

Source: Population census, Republic of Slovenia Bureau of Statistics

The socio-economic development of Slovenia in the post-war period went through some characteristic phases (Klemenčić, 1989). The agrarian phase lasted up until the 1960s, when the predominant share of the working population was employed in primary production. The industrial phase lasted from the 1960s to the 1990s, when the share of the population in secondary production was as high as 50 per cent. The tertiary or post-industrial phase from 1990 onwards marks the phase when the percentage of the working population employed in secondary production was beginning to drop. A leading role has been taken on by the tertiary sector, while the share of the working population employed in primary production has stagnated at approximately 13 per cent.

The Spatial Development of the Socio-Economic Structure

The economic development of Slovenia to date and the influences of the neighbouring macroeconomic systems are clearly reflected in the regionally varying socio-economic structures. Post-war spatial development of these structures has the following characteristics (Klemenčić, 1993).

In the 1950s the majority of the working population was employed in the primary sector on three-quarters of Slovenian territory. On the remaining quarter employment in secondary activities predominated as a consequence of the penetration of industrialization from Austria in the second half of the nineteenth century and the development of industry during the inter-war period, in large part through the assistance of Czech capital.

By the 1990s large-scale industrialization had taken place in Slovenia. Only one quarter of the territory was characterized by a predominance of employment in the primary sector, in the north-east and east along the border with Hungary and Croatia. From its core areas the secondary sector rapidly expanded to rural areas. In the south-west of Slovenia, especially along the coast, the tertiary sector was already beginning to dominate. Thus in this period of recent Slovene economic history three types of socio-economic structures co-existed, which also developed under the influence of three economic systems: Yugoslav, as reflected in rapid industrialization; the Eastern (centrally planned) model, which indirectly through the closing of the border had an influence on the north-eastern part of Slovenia in terms of its lack of development; and the Western influence, which especially along the border with Italy promoted the growth of tertiary activities.

In the 1990s Slovenia experienced a qualitative jump in socio-economic development. The region where the primary sector remained dominant was still retained only in the extreme north-eastern part of the country, while the region with a predominant tertiary sector expanded to a third of the state territory.

With respect to the post-war socio-economic development of Slovenia we could divide the country into three main regions:

(a) A region of permanent backwardness in terms of socio-economic development, below the Slovene average, which extends through the north-eastern and eastern part of the country along the border with Hungary and Croatia.

(b) A region ahead of the average level of development. On the whole this applies to the area along the Southern Railway between Vienna and Trieste. This transportation axis acted as a major stimulus to the development of industrialization in the second half of the nineteenth century.

(c) The remaining region, which after the Second World War became fairly well industrialized but has not been successful in restructuring in the last decade.

Unemployment as a New Social Problem

Certain structural changes in industry as a result of political changes in the 1990s can be perceived through trends in the numbers of people employed in industrial sectors. A comparison of the number of employed workers in the most important industrial sectors between 1989 and 1993 reveals the following picture.

The number of workers in ferrous metallurgy and machine-building declined by 45 per cent. The number of workers in metal-processing, electrical machine production and furniture manufacturing fell by 35 per cent. It is interesting to note that the drop in the number of workers in the textile industry was relatively small (13 per cent) and that this sector in large part carried the burden of the first shock which the Slovene economy experienced at the beginning of the 1990s as a result of the loss of the Yugoslav market.

A comparison of the trends in the numbers of workers according to employment sector between the first half of 1993 and 1994 shows a slowing of changes. The level of reduction of workers is usually no greater than 20 per cent; machine-building, production of basic chemicals, forestry, transport and communications, small businesses and research activities are among the areas most affected. The greatest increases in employment were in ferrous metallurgy (7 per cent), real estate and personal insurance (12 per cent), low-rise construction (18 per cent) and personal services (20 per cent). Increase in the number of employed in ferrous metallurgy in 1994 as compared with 1993 is merely a consolidation of conditions, after a severe contraction in the number of employed at the beginning of the 1990s. The continuation of motorway construction in Slovenia gave a strong impetus to the construction sector, which had been hard hit.

Due to the above-mentioned changes in the structure of employment a relatively new problem has arisen: unemployment. From a hardly noticeable level of 1.5 per cent in 1987, unemployment rose to 14 per cent in 1993. Later statistics have shown that growth in unemployment has stopped and that the level even dropped slightly in some months.

The levels of unemployment according to commune are very changeable. A number of plants have gone bankrupt as a result of pressure by individuals or groups who benefit from the artificially induced drop in value of the company in the privatization process. In some cases, privatization is also carried out via a by-pass firm, which can also increase the number of unemployed, at least temporarily.

Thus it is difficult to read common characteristics in the development of unemployment in communes. Most strongly affected is the Maribor industrial region, which is mostly extensive in nature and operates using outdated technology. The rest of the industrial axis of central Slovenia is also considerably affected. Outside this region a high level of unemployment (15 per cent) is found in communes bordering Croatia, which industrialized rapidly in the 1970s.

Changes in the Ethnic Composition of the Population

Post-war industrialization in Slovenia attracted workers from the other republics of Yugoslavia. By far the greatest numbers of workers came from less developed regions, who were in the main unskilled workers. They found jobs in industrial enterprises, construction and municipal services. Their main destinations were industrial and mining regions, Ljubljana and the border regions, to which the population from the neighbouring border regions of Croatia emigrated.

The presence of such a large share of foreign workers has caused numerous problems, similar to those in Western European countries. For example, in Slovenia, as in some Western European countries, there was a concentration of foreign workers in old urban centres. The young domestic population began moving out of old apartments in city centres in the late 1960s and moved to new apartment complexes on the edges of the city. In a number of Slovene cities the older urban cores were characterized by a number of foreign, usually younger, inhabitants and older domestic residents (Klemenčić, 1993). In the city of Jesenice, with its steel mill, 37 per cent of the population were of non-Slovene origin; other cities such as Velenje, Koper, Tržič and Portorož had shares of 27–29 per cent, and even Ljubljana had a share of 22 per cent.

The arrival of foreigners changed the ethnic composition of the population. In 1953 the proportion of ethnic Slovenes was 96.5 per cent. The autochthonous Italian and Hungarian minorities accounted for 0.8 per cent, while the remainder were for the most part immigrants from other Yugoslav republics. In 1991 the latter accounted for 7 per cent while the proportion of ethnic Slovenes declined to 87.8 per cent.

In six communes, more than 25 per cent of the population are of non-Slovene origin. This is an extremely high proportion for Slovenia, which was an unusually homogeneous republic until fairly recently. Slovenes living in these areas often feel threatened, which is also a result of the small size of the Slovene nation generally and a feeling of being threatened by much larger neighbouring peoples. Of the six Slovene communes mentioned, three lie along the border with Italy and one along the border with Hungary. In all four of these communes inhabitants who emigrated from other parts of Yugoslavia add substantially to the share of the non-Slovene population. The other two communes, with the highest proportion of non-Slovene population, are Jesenice and Ljubljana: the first attracted foreign workers to the steel mill and the second to construction.

In spite of legislation restricting the employment of foreigners, in 1994 about 20,000 foreigners, of whom 90 per cent were from former Yugoslav republics, were granted work permits. The majority of these workers, who represent about 2.5 per cent of the total active population, perform menial and low-paid jobs shunned by Slovenes. This reflects the relatively high level of socio-economic development achieved by Slovenia in comparison with the other republics of Yugoslavia.

Urbanization as a Reflection of Socio-Economic Development

The level of urbanization in Slovenia is unusually low at 50 per cent, but should not be interpreted as a reflection of the level of socio-economic development. After the Second World War, settlement in Slovenia passed through all levels. Initial concentration of the population in republic centres was followed by the concept of polycentric development, which encouraged the development of a number of regional centres.

The proximity of industrial centres, the development of industrialization and the simultaneous development of private car traffic, as well as the strong attachment of Slovenes to a rural environment, impeded the development of classic urbanization. In the period 1971–81 more than half of all Slovene towns were growing in population and only 10 per cent were losing population. In the 1990s the suburbs of Slovene cities experienced demographic growth, while there was a strong decrease in population growth of cities (Ravbar, 1992).

Table 5.4 The development of urbanization in Slovenia

Year	1961	1971	1981	1991
%	36.1	44.6	48.9	50.5

Strong urbanization took place in slightly more than a quarter of Slovene cities, moderate growth in slightly more than half, and weak growth in a fifth of city suburbs. Ravbar has defined three different types of city suburbs (Ravbar, 1992):

(a) Polycentric urban regions with a high degree of suburbanization and usually the result of larger suburbs merging with one another. These regions have developed in the vicinity of Ljubljana, coastal cities,

Celje and Maribor. These are also regions which have achieved the highest level of socio-economic development, usually in the tertiary sector.

(b) Monocentric highly suburbanized but isolated regions. The majority of Slovene towns fall into this category, but have varying effects on their hinterlands.

(c) Weakly suburbanized regions around small cities in economically less developed regions, which are frequently still sparsely populated (karst regions), such that it is questionable as to whether suburbanization is really the right word to use.

According to Ravbar's investigations there are 167 suburbanized regions which include one eighth of the land area, a third of the settlements and three-quarters of the population (Ravbar, 1992).

Thus Slovenia very rapidly underwent the first level of urbanization in a somewhat milder form and in the 1990s found itself in the phase of spatial development of urbanization as experienced by the most economically developed countries.

Concluding Remarks

The present-day economic structure of Slovenia is the result of three major phases of economic development within the framework of three different countries: the Austrian monarchy before the First World War, the Kingdom of Yugoslavia between the wars and socialist Yugoslavia after the Second World War.

The socio-economic transformation of Slovene society after the Second World War developed relatively slowly and organically. A major weakness of socio-economic development was the above-average share of the population employed in industry. It could be said that the socio-economic development of Slovenia after the last war contained elements of the development of Western capitalist countries, as seen in the increase of the share of tertiary sector activities since the 1980s, and of that of the Eastern socialist countries, as reflected (particularly from the 1960s to the 1980s) in the high share of the industrial population.

Political changes and the declaration of independence did not represent a shock for the Slovene economy in structural terms. The biggest problem was the sudden halt in exports to the republics of former Yugoslavia, although this had the advantage of stimulating the economy to a more rapid restructuring. The emigration of a portion of foreign workers from the republics of former Yugoslavia alleviated somewhat the level of unemployment caused by the loss of the Yugoslav market.

Slovenia is meeting the new challenges offered by international co-operation and integration. The decisions on how Slovenia will be included in the European and world communities will be recorded in the socio-economic and spatial development of Slovenia. Natural advantages and development to date argue in favour of sustainable development which would take into account the regional diversity and small size of Slovenia.

References

Klemenčić, Marijan M. (1989), 'Družbenogospodarski prehod v Sloveniji', *Dela*, 6, pp. 230-40.

Klemenčić, Marijan M. (1993a), 'Starostna in narodnostna sestava prebivalcev Tržiča', *Geografski vestnik*, 65, pp. 79-90.

Klemenčić, Marijan M. (1993b), 'Družbenogospodarski razvoj obmejnih obomočij v Sloveniji', *Dela*, 10, pp. 127-34.

Population censuses of 1953, 1961, 1971, 1981, 1991. Republic of Slovenia Bureau of Statistics, Ljubljana.

Ravbar, M. (1992), *Suburbanizacija v Sloveniji*, Filozofska fakulteta, Ljubljana.

Statistical information 1994, Republic of Slovenia Bureau of Statistics, Ljubljana.

Statistical Yearbook of the Republic of Slovenia 1993, Republic of Slovenia Bureau of Statistics, Ljubljana.

6 The Resurgence of Submerged Minorities: Hungarians and Italians in Slovenia

ANDRÉ-LOUIS SANGUIN

The European state of the Republic of Slovenia, with a population of two million (1993 estimate), covers a territory of 20,256 square kilometres. The Slovene people voted for independence from Yugoslavia in the referendum of 23 December 1990, and on 25 June 1991 the Slovene Parliament declared the Republic of Slovenia a sovereign state. The Constitution was proclaimed on 23 December 1991. So from the ashes of former Yugoslavia a new country has emerged on the world's political map. From Yugoslavia, Slovenia inherits the socio-geographic conditions of two territories settled by national minorities: the Italians along the Adriatic Coast and the Hungarians along the north-east corner (see Figure 6.1).

Historical Minorities at Slovene Border Edges

Slovenia was always located at the European ethnic crossroads and its position was one of a zone of transit. Until 1918, the present Slovene state territory was part of the Habsburg Empire. The Slovenia of the time, together with other South Slav remnants of the Austro-Hungarian Empire, joined the new Kingdom of Yugoslavia. But according to the Rapallo Treaty (1920) a large part of western Slovenia was ceded to Italy, including all of Slovene Istria. From 1420 to 1797, the present Slovene Istria was part of the Venetian Republic. This extended historical period explains the importance of Italian cultural and linguistic features in Slovene Istria. From 1797 to 1918, Istria was ruled by Austria, but the Italian language and culture remained and were respected.

From 1920 to 1945, the whole of Istria was part of Italy and inhabited by approximately 300,000 Italians (the Fascist dictatorship inflated the census results). After the Second World War and the strange political experience of the Free Territory of Trieste (1947–54), the Italian-speaking population in

Slovene Istria was involved in a great exodus towards Italy. Italians numbered 21,741 in Slovene Istria in 1948, falling to 2,622 in 1961. In 1954, a new international boundary between Italy and Yugoslavia caused major changes for the Italian minority in areas which became part of what was then Yugoslavia. A great deal of these Italians moved to Italy and many even went overseas, both because of the border changes and also because of the pressure put on them by Yugoslavian and Italian propaganda. The immigration of the Italian minority after the Second World War caused great changes in the national structure of Istria. It is estimated that approximately 22,500 residents of Istria, Rijeka, Kvarner and the Kvarner Islands left these territories.

The story of Hungarians in Slovenia is less complicated because, in 1918, the international boundary between Hungary and Yugoslavia was established according to the *uti posidetis* principle: the former internal boundary between the late Habsburg Empire's territories became an international boundary. The ethnic structure was changed in the 1920s as the Serbian-led kingdom replaced the rulers from Vienna. Slovenes decided to colonize the pre-First World War Hungarian part of the Monarchy, the Prekmurje, where the German-speaking population decreased from 4,775 in 1910 to just eighty in 1991. From 1948 (Yugoslav secession from Cominform) to 1961, because of the Iron Curtain, all communication between the Hungarian-speaking minority and Hungary itself was almost totally cut. From 1961 to 1989, the border between Yugoslavia and Hungary stayed relatively closed. North-eastern Slovenia had an unconnected settlement of Hungarian minority in ethnically mixed villages, economically removed and underdeveloped. Because of the above, and in preserving the aged farming population and the low level of professional and educational structures, the Hungarian minority was much more subject to depopulation, displacement and assimilation.

By 1910, the Prekmurje region had 14,637 Hungarian-speaking citizens; by 1931, there were 7,407 Hungarians (40 per cent of the Prekmurje ethnic structure). The numerical size of the Hungarian ethnicity has since remained unchanged, and their relative decline (to 8.5 per cent of the regional population) has its grounds in urban development and Slovene immigration.

A study of mixed nationality areas in Prekmurje and Kopersko Primorje (Slovene Istria) has to take into account the degree of socio-economic integrity and the percentage of mixed marriages. Every ethnic territory followed different paths of development. Northern Istria was influenced by Koper harbour activity and international tourism along the Slovene Riviera. The Hungarian Prekmurje remained underdeveloped until just over two decades ago. The 1971 and 1981 censuses have shown that bilingual education increased the number of mixed marriages.

Italian-speaking workers in Istria are more involved in quaternary activities than the local Slovenes. In Prekmurje, the Hungarian population structure changed, basically because of migration from rural to industrial jobs, mainly in Salovci, Murska Sobota, Lendava and Prosenjakovci. The highly skilled Hungarian population moved to Murska Sobota.

Prekmurje (Transmuraland): Hungarian-Speaking Region in the Former Communist Slovenia

The Hungarian-speaking area in Prekmurje ('Transmuraland', or the area located north-eastwards from the Mura river) extends along the formerly closed Yugoslav–Hungarian border. The major part of this area belongs to the territory of two communes, Murska Sobota and Lendava. In the middle are two Slovene-populated areas, Kobilje and Strehovci. The two commune territories are very different. Murska Sobota has no central location for Hungarians and is made up of eleven Hungarian-speaking centres. The area of Lendava/Lendva gravitates to the communal centre, under the influence of a speed-up development with favorable conditions: traffic situation, opportunities for farming, jobs in non-agrarian occupations. The Lendava area is made up of twenty-two Hungarian-speaking centres along the foothills of Lendavske Gorice.

The area of Prekmurje exhibits negative features in economic development and the structure of population (60 per cent of the population in agrarian jobs and a decrease in the number of Hungarians), mainly in the hilly sections. The clearly peripheral position (less favourable for farming) and economic underdevelopment have led to emigration from this area. The border with Croatia has attracted some Croatian population. According to the 1981 census, 15,101 people lived in Prekmurje (2,046 in the eleven locations of the Murska Sobota commune and 13,055 in the twenty-two locations of the Lendava commune). Compared with the 1961 and 1971 censuses, Murska Sobota is on the decline and Lendava largely in stagnation. The number of Hungarians in both areas is in retrogression because of low natural increase: 10,395 in 1953 but 8,503 in 1991. Cultural traditions mean the tendency of demographic ageing is particulary marked among the Hungarian minority in Prekmurje.

When analysing the educational level of the Hungarian minority living in Prekmurje, one has to consider not only the dichotomy between village and town but, first and foremost, comparisons with Slovene inhabitants. The educational differences are due not only to the ethnic differences but also to socio-economic and demographic features. The Hungarians have remained a much more agrarian population, whereas the Slovenes have a considerably higher degree of spatial and social mobility. Before the establishment of bilingual classrooms, Hungarian children in the countryside attended only Hungarian classes, depriving them of the chance for further education and better employment.

There is a considerable difference between the economic level of the two communes. The most dynamic and vital section is Lendava, the only urban settlement. The reason for the underdevelopment of the Murska Sobota area lies in the local distance from the only bigger urban centre of Murska Sobota.

The mixed Hungarian–Slovene households are the sector of the population with a relatively higher education while members of purely Hungarian households have the lowest degree of education. In terms of professional skills, the differences between the Slovene and Hungarian populations are considerable, and certainly due to the socio-economic factors paralled by those in educational differences. The high percentage of Hungarian workers active in the primary sector is also a chief characteristic.

Landownership is the domain of the Hungarian autochthonous population. This leads to better opportunities for preserving both the national identity and a fairly compact territory. The authochthonous Hungarian population lives in the areas along the Hungarian border, with the exception of Kobilje, which since the First World War has been settled by Slovenes. This involved an encroachment upon the land of Hungarians. The other route by which the Slovene population has grown is the older and more frequent tradition of nationally mixed weddings. At Centiba (the most south-easternward corner of Prekmurje, wedged between Hungary and Croatia), 70.4 per cent of households are pure Hungarian, 19.9 per cent are mixed Hungarian–Slovene and 9.7 per cent are pure Slovene.

Kopersko Primorje (Slovene Istria): Italian-Speaking Region in the Former Communist Slovenia

The Slovene Istria (or Kopersko Primorje) is also the second ethno-linguistic mixed area in Slovenia. This too is a more complicated border region than Prekmurje because it lies along the open Italian–Slovene border and the new international Croatian–Slovene border. The Italian-speaking area of Slovenia is entirely located within the so-called Slovene Riviera. Lying between Italy and Croatia, it is the single maritime window, with a coastline just forty-six kilometres long.

Slovene Istria has had a turbulent historical past, the change of political power being the basic characteristic of its historical development. From 1813 to 1918, Slovene Istria was part of the Habsburg Empire. From 1920 to 1945, the territory became a part of Italy. After 1945, it was ceded to Yugoslavia. After the Second World War, the change of the political border decisively influenced the new distribution of the Italian-speaking population. Today, the population of Italian origin lives on places close to the coast and included in the three Slovene coastal communes (Koper, Izola, Piran). In the commune of Koper/Capodistria, Italians live in twenty-five areas; in Piran/Pirano, in eight areas; and in Izola/Isola, in five coastal areas. The Italian population rapidly decreased after the Second World War and mainly after the end of the period of the Free Territory of Trieste (1947–54). By 1948, the Italian population numbered 21,336 in forty-seven locations in Slovene Istria. By 1961, the Italian population was only 3,072, in thirty-eight Primorje areas. By the first Slovene census of 1991, they numbered 3,064.

In the early years after the Second World War, the houses vacated by Italians were taken up by the population from other parts of Slovenia and from the coastal hinterland of Croatia. Between the censuses of 1961 and 1991, the percentage of linguistically mixed households declined. The Primorje Italian-speaking population stands out by its small spatial mobility: 50 per cent came from Italy before the Second World War and a substantial number from Croatian Istria after the Second World War. The age structure of the population of Italian origin is characterized by the ageing of the population (28.9 per cent are over sixty). Also characteristic is the employment structure of the Italians: 13.4 per cent in primary sectors versus 4.2 per cent regional average, but 36.1 per cent in quaternary sectors versus 23.8 per cent regional average. The high percentage of active Italians in the quaternary sector doubtless results from specific jobs in educational, administrative and media organs (radio, television, school, cultural centres and so on). Until the collapse of Communism and the emergence of an independent Republic of Slovenia, the most noticeable demographic feature of the Italians in Primorje was a strong relative and absolute numerical decline.

In Primorje's Italian-speaking areas, it often happened that the population did not state its origin by nationality. As regards the subjective decision for declaring national provenance, there are many dilemmas, particulary in the case of nationally mixed marriages. In other words, because of the Communist system, many Italians hid their ethnic origin. Also, they were flooded by the main stream of immigrants: from inner Slovenia in the first fifteen years after the war and from Yugoslavia in the seventies. Within Primorje, migrations of the Italian minority had a much more local character, determined by the processes of urbanization, deagrarianization and industrialization. In the fishing harbours located along Slovene Riviera, many fishermen rely heavily on the Italian minority.

Until the independence of Slovenia (1991), negative tendencies in the development of the Italian community had been noted (ageing of the Italian population, growing mumber of ethnically mixed marriages, fear of the declaring ethnicity at the time of Communist census). This situation is over. This is clearly obvious from the fact that non-Italian parents have started sending their children to schools with Italian as the language of instruction. Now, seven-tenths of people declare themselves to be Italians by mother tongue. The overall knowledge of Italian is quite widespread. From some surveys, it appears that Italian is spoken by seven-tenths of the Kopersko Primorje population and Italian or Slovene by two-thirds.

The Resurgence of Submerged Communities in the New Slovenia

The constitution of the Republic of Slovenia guarantees special rights to the Italian and Hungarian minorities. The most important of these are:

(1) In ethnically-mixed territories, Slovene and the language of the minority are equal. All public services are bilingual.
(2) Free use of national symbols; establisment of autonomous organizations and institutions.
(3) Development of information networks in the minorities' own language.
(4) Development of school networks in Hungarian and in Italian.
(5) Direct representation in the Slovene Parliament.

In recent years, the Italian minority has placed special emphasis on economic development, realizing that having its own economic basis should make its existence easier. A number of projects are being prepared in which the Italian government is participating. The Hungarian minority bases its aspirations for the future on the faster development of the border regions as a whole and anticipates consultative and material assistance in the preparation of development plans in which the construction of transportation and telecom-munications networks will be given special emphasis.

In the framework of the joint Italian Union Organization, the Italian minority is establishing close links with the Italian minority in Croatia, with whom it shares a common fate and many common organizations and institutions. The Italian Union is also a link to Italy. Italy has extended greater assistance to the Italian minority since Slovene independence. Lately, Hungary has been paying more attention to its minority in Slovenia and has established rather close ties with it. In November 1992, Hungary and Slovenia signed a special agreement on the protection of the Hungarian minority in Slovenia and of the Slovene minority in Hungary.

Article 64 of the Slovene Constitution provides special rights to Italian and Hungarian ethnic minorities. Their realization is morally and materially supported by the state, which should also assure the minorities' participation in the political system at all levels. Every ethnic community has one deputy in the National Assembly. Politically, both the Italian and Hungarian ethnic communities are organized in self-governing associations which serve as their basic political organizations. Special electoral lists are compiled in the areas where these two communities exist (Koper/Capodistria, Piran/Pirano, Izola/Isola, Murska Sobota, Lendava/Lendva). The Slovene Parliament has a Special Commission for the Italian and Hungarian ethnic communities which deals with issues concerning them. In the ethnically mixed regions, bilingualism is guaranteed in all branches of the judiciary system.

Due to various historical circumstances and socio-demographic conditions, as well as by international arrangement, two models of bilingual education are practiced in the ethnically mixed areas of Slovenia. Both are maintenance/enrichment models, their social goal being cultural pluralism and their linguistic goal bilingualism: minority and majority members are given the opportunity to develop at least a receptive competence in the other group's language. A bilingual educational system has existed in Prekmurje since 1959. All children (Slovene and Hungarian) attend mixed classes. In 1991–92, there were 1,408 pupils in ten bilingual primary schools and the single bilingual secondary school was attended by 312 pupils. In accordance with the 1954 London Memorandum and the Slovene–Italian agreement of 1992, educational institutions in Primorje (Slovene Istria), from kindergartens to colleges, are monolingual, with either Slovene or Italian as the language of instruction. In 1991–92, there were nine Italian primary schols attended by 516 pupils and three Italian secondary schools attended by 233 pupils.

The cultural organization of the two ethnic communities is represented by various educational and cultural institutions (schools, libraries, museums and so on), publications in the mother tongue and radio and television networks. In Primorje (Istria) many Italian cultural groups operate within the framework of the Comunità degli Italiani. There are more than fifty cultural groups of the Hungarian community in Prekmurje. Radio Koper/Capodistria began broadcasting in Italian in 1945; TV Koper/Capodistria has broadcast since 1971 and serves as the television station of the Italian minorities in Slovenia and Croatia. Radio Lendava/Lendva broadcasts in Hungarian about seven hours a day. A team of Hungarian editors in Lendava/Lendva works within RTV Slovenia to produce a special programme every two weeks.

Conclusion: A European Laboratory at the Crossroads of Three Cultures

Located at the crossroads of three great neighbouring cultures (German, Latin, Slavic), Slovenia is not only one of the smallest but also one of the youngest of the European countries. With the increasingly intensified development of Slovenia's border roles and border regions, and the linking of these with the border regions of neighbouring countries, opportunities have been opened to Slovene minorities in neighbouring countries (Porabje in Hungary, Friuli-Venezia Giulia in Italy, Carinthia and Styria in Austria) as well as to the Italian and Hungarian minorities in Slovenia, to assure their role as intermediaries between Slovenia and its neighbours in economic, cultural and other human activities. The intercultural upbringing of the general Slovene population and of its minorities and the high degree of legal protection for the rights of ethnic minorities in Slovenia guarantees a functional bilingualism in all ethnically mixed areas so that each group can use its own language and still get along well with the others.

It is important to stress that the constitutional order of the new Slovenia recognizes the superiority of accepted international legal obligations over internal legislation regarding minority rights. Several international monitoring missions have already confirmed that ethnic minorities in Slovenia are protected even better than international standards demand.

In this century, Slovenia has suffered considerable changes in its state borders. Within the framework of the former Yugoslavia, from the sixties onwards, the political geography of Slovenia began to be strenghtened because the Iron Curtain had begun opening a good thirty years earlier than in other Communist countries and the other Yugoslav republics. In the process of opening and linking neighbouring countries and regions within the framework of the Alpe-Adria Euroregion, the Hungarian and Italian minorities, with their knowledge of the languages of two neighbouring countries, shoulder an increasing importance. For these reasons, Italian and Hungarian minorities in Slovenia represent significant areas within the Alpe-Adria Euroregion.

Finally, it is possible to learn a triptych geopolitical lesson from the Slovene case-study:

(1) With barely 12,000 people constituting the Hungarian and Italian minorities for a country of two million people, Slovenia is doing better than many other European countries facing similar ethnic problems.

(2) Compared with other former Communist Eastern European countries, the situation of ethnic minorities in Slovenia is at the top. The Hungarian minority in Slovenia enjoys a socio-economic

environment diametrically opposed to that prevailing for the Hungarians in Romania and Slovakia.

(3) Compared with some European Union countries like France, Slovenia was able to reject the barren Jacobin sight and to bring construction and bright settlements to the challenge of ethnic minorities.

Finally, the best compliment awarded to Slovenia is, paradoxically, the reproach made by the Council of Europe. Indeed, by giving a minority status to its 3,000 Italians and its 9,000 Hungarians, representing less than 1 per cent of its population, Slovenia was criticized, at the moment of its admission to the Council of Europe in 1993, since it created here a 'precedent excessively liberal'!

References

Bufon, Milan (1993), 'Istra: novi problemi starih regig/Istria: i nuovi problemi delle antiche regioni', *Annales*, no. 3, pp.197–202.

Colummi, Cristiana et al. (1980), *Storia di un esodo, Istria 1945–1956*, Trieste.

Darovec, Darko (1993), *Rassegna di storia istriana*, Koper.

Gosar, Anton (1993), 'Nationalities of Slovenia, Changing Ethnic Structures in Central Europe', *GeoJournal*, vol. 30, no. 3, pp. 215–23.

Klemenčić, Vladimir (1985), 'Situazione delle nazionalita italiana ed ungherese e territori di nazionalita mista nell'Istria slovena e nell'Oltramura (Pomurje) dal punto di vista della geografia sociale', *Geographica Slovenica*, no. 16, pp. 129–36.

Klemenčić, Vladimir (1993), 'National Minorities as an Element of the Demographic and Spatial Structure of the Alpine-Adriatic-Pannonian Region', *GeoJournal*, vol. 30, no. 3, pp. 207–14.

Klemenčić, Vladimir and Genorio, Rado (1993), 'The New State of Slovenia and Its Function within the Frame of Europe', *GeoJournal*, vol. 30, no. pp. 323–33.

Klopčić, Vera and Stergar, Janez (1993), *Ethnic Minorities in Slovenia*, Ljubljana, Institute for Ethnic Studies.

Milani-Kruljac, Nelida (1990), 'La communita italiana in Istria e a Fiume fra diglossia e bilinguismo', *Etnia*, no. 1, pp. 1–250.

O'Loughlin, John and Van der Wusten, Herman (1993), *The New Political Geography of Eastern Europe*, London.

Pak, Mirko (ed.) (1992), *Slovenia, Geographical Aspects of a New Independent European Nation*, Ljubljana.

Piry, Ivo and Repolusk, Peter (1985), 'Territorio di nazionalita mista dell'Istria slovena', *Geographica Slovenica*, no. 16, pp. 137–68.

Philippart, Eric (ed.) (1993), *Nations et frontières dans la nouvelle Europe*, Brussels.

Van Amersfoort, Hans and Knippenberg, Hans (1991), *States and Nations, The Rebirth of the Nationalities Question in Europe*, Netherlands Geographical Studies 137, Amsterdam.

Verne, Etienne (1986), 'La Situation de l'enseignement bilingue dans la République de Slovénie', in *Education in Multilingual Societies*, Institute for Ethnic Studies, Ljubljana, pp. 102–13.

7 Industrial Restructuring Through Privatization: Evidence from Romania

CLAUDIA POPESCU

In 1989, industry in socialist Romania had three outstanding characteristics. The first was an even distribution of industrial capacities throughout the national territory. Reflecting the former economic inequalities between the main historical regions of the country and combined with a desire to demonstrate the superiority of the system, socialist economic policy was founded on the principle of equity and territorial harmony. So, with a poor perception of space and highly subsidized transport costs, location decisions brought industry to all parts of the country. With some ideologically inspired manipulation, statistical data showed increasing equality in industrial output between counties. This objective was given such priority in the 1970s and 1980s that a fixed volume of industrial output was extracted from each county with no regard to the industrial structure, the number of employees required or the value-added. Paradoxically, however, some industrial investments were allocated to the counties according to their importance — which tended to exaggerate those regional imbalances that still existed.

A second characteristic, fully expressed under socialist policy, was the comprehensive, 'many-sided' nature of the industrialization programme. Extending the idea of economic self-sufficiency from the national to the regional level, each county was to produce everything it needed. So, regional specialization of industry was replaced by the aim of a diversified industrial profile. The number of specialized industrial centres fell from 104 in 1965 to fifty-seven in 1989. There were also changes in structure, with an increasing role for heavy industry. Thus, whereas in 1965 the food industry had the greatest share of the total production (25.0 per cent), at the end of the socialist period its place was taken by engineering. Developed at a rapid pace, industry was the pivotal element of the national economy, with entirely state-owned enterprises recruiting the vast labour force generated by the collectivization of agriculture. This transfer of labour not only explains the decline of rural settlement in general and agricultural activity in particular, but the rapid urbanization process as well. The fundamental role of industry in urban growth is shown by the prominence of the industrial towns within the functional urban structure.

The third characteristic was the growing importance of large industrial enterprises. The increasing size of the average industrial unit (500 employees in 1965; 2,500 in 1989) meant rapid urban growth; about two-thirds of the recent urban growth has been provided by the rural population. The most recent trend of industrial evolution has been to concentrate the productive activities in ever bigger industrial units. In 1989, enterprises with more than 5,000 employees accounted for 37.4 per cent of the industrial workforce, 9.7 per cent of the total number of enterprises and 35.4 per cent of the national output. Economies of scale having no relevance for the functional dimension of industry, the big enterprises represented all industrial branches and were located in different towns irrespective of their size. The majority of towns increased their population three or four times under socialism as they accommodated huge industrial enterprises. As a consequence, the larger towns became increasingly important. In 1992 the twenty-five largest towns (around 10 per cent of the total number) comprised 57.5 per cent of the urban population and 56.1 per cent of the urban industrial workforce.

The Evolution of the Spatial Pattern

In spite of the location policy, some regional differences remained, showing discrepancies between the ideological principle and the real potential of each area. The share of the industrial workforce among the total active population at the communal level shows considerable variation. Regions such as Moldavia, Oltenia or Dobrogea, which were formerly backward, remain relatively unimportant in relation to the main axis of industrial development, linking Transylvania with Muntenia, which was already prominent before the Second World War. These regional imbalances, however, are not so great as before and they present opportunities for further development. The present evolution shows a strong spatial selectivity caused by: (1) the change of logic and the abandonment of the central political decision-making process; (2) the emergence of new industrial processes — conversion, decentralization, privatization and foreign capital inflow, with corresponding spatial responses; (3) the replacement of the general environment of slow economic growth registered before 1989 with a period of economic crisis; and (4) the increasing number of decision-makers: enterprises, private entrepreneurs and local communities, with conflicting or interdependent interests. The importance of the local initiative will emphasize the regional disparities.

Under socialism, industry was the most important branch of the Romanian economy and it registered continuous growth. But today the trend is one of decline: between 1989 and 1992 the industrial workforce lost 660,000 employees (17.8 per cent of the total) while industrial output halved. At the regional level it is evident that the greater the importance of industry the greater the losses among the labour force. Thus the greatest decreases in the industrial workforce have been registered in the western and central regions of the country. In the eastern and southern regions, meanwhile, there are relatively small losses and even gains in some cases. The only significant growth, however, is experienced by the regions dominated by the mining industry and the metropolitan region of Bucharest.

Industrial Restructuring: The Key Economic Process of the Transition Period

The most complex and difficult economic process of the present transition period is industrial restructuring. In 1989 industry was the main economic branch, employing 38.1 per cent of the workforce, compared with only 12.0 per cent in 1950. Ninety-five per cent of industry was located in the towns and so it is in the urban areas where restructuring is most important, providing the key for reinvigoration of the economy as a whole. The former relationships have changed, for management is no longer centrally controlled, while the collapse of Comecon meant the loss of traditional markets. At the same time some products proved uncompetitive in Western markets and the practice of dumping goods on foreign markets, much used by the Communist government, was largely curtailed. The iron and steel, engineering and chemical industries, which were far too large for the national market and inadequately structured for international competition, reduced output by between 40 and 60 per cent in 1992 as against 1989 levels. With a lack of capable managers and a well thought-out transition strategy, there was an increase in unemployment, which eventually affected about 11.5 per cent of the active population.

Industrial restructuring affected all the towns, but the large cities were most easily able to absorb factory workers in the service activities that were substantially undersized by Western European standards The small and medium towns, relying heavily on one or two big enterprises, faced serious social challenges when enterprises were forced to close. In some small towns some 75–90 per cent of the industrial workforce may be employed in one huge enterprise. Temporary social protection solutions have had some ameliorative effect, but the situation remains difficult, with high ‘technical unemployment’ as workers remain on the books but take time off on a rotation basis. Towns concerned with light industry and food industries linked closely with local resources are in a better situation. Some, however, have been affected by the privatization of agriculture and the alarming reduction of industrial crops (sunflower, sugar beet and soya) as private farmers are attracted by more profitable enterprises. Demand for fertilizer has fallen sharply, with farmers unable to afford it. But the small and medium industrial centres based on wood-processing units enjoy secure markets at home and abroad (especially for furniture), so employment has been retained and some additional employees have been taken on.

The Land Law of 1991 adversely affected industrial activities in some small towns (especially towns in the plain and hill regions with a poorly developed industrial sector) when inhabitants became landowners and preferred to work in agriculture. But it is also true that in large cities the rural commuters seeking an extra source of income were the first to lose their jobs. The UN embargo against the former Yugoslavia also had a negative effect on Romanian industry, especially in the towns situated along the Danube. During the three years to 1994 they lost up to 60 per cent of their industrial workforce.

Fortunately, however, the continuous decline in the proportion of the active population employed in manufacturing between 1990 and 1992 does not extend to other sections of industry, such as mining and electricity and gas and water. Here there has been an increase from 3.6 to 4.2 per cent (see Table 7.1). For industry as a whole, however, the employment share has fallen from 37.9 to 31.6 per cent. It is clear that at the moment industrial restructuring requires huge financial and social efforts, which at the moment Romania cannot afford because it has neither the economic capacity nor the managerial expertise and domestic capital. Therefore the limited endogenous development potential must be complemented by foreign investment to introduce new organizational forms of labour, new products and new markets. At the same time, the replacement of state property with private ownership will call for new attitudes which will pose another challenge for the transition period.

Table 7.1 Romania: share of the active population employed in industry, 1990–92

	Percentage of the total active population employed		
	1990	1991	1992
Industry as a whole	37.9	35.3	31.6
Mining	2.4	2.6	2.6
Manufacturing	34.3	31.3	27.4
Electricity, Gas and Water	1.2	1.4	1.6

Geographical Features of the Privatization Process

One of the major processes going on now is privatization. This plays a vital role during the transition because it implies the accomplishment of two of the most difficult changes: behavioural and organizational. A change of attitude towards work is needed, including stronger worker responsibility and participation. New forms of industrial work organization should emerge, ensuring flexibility of production and efficient management of the labour force. Privatization involves the transfer of ownership from the state to private owners. It can be achieved by large-scale 'big' privatization relating to domestic capital or alternatively by the inflow of foreign investments expressed through joint ventures. The former was provided for under Law 58 of August 1991, stipulating the transfer of 30 per cent of the nominal share capital in commercial companies to eligible Romanian citizens. Transfer was to be achieved by the free distribution of Ownership Certificates to the 16.5 million people involved. Five Private Ownership Funds were set up as joint-stock companies able to issue Certificates of Ownership, seek to maximize profits accruing to the holders of Certificates of Ownership and develop methods for using the Certificates of Ownership to acquire shares in commercial companies. The holders had the right to buy and sell certificates and to exchange them for shares at any company being privatized within a period of not more than five years. The administration and the selling of shares and assets was to be undertaken by the State Ownership Fund, whose initial share of 70 per cent of the nominal capital of commercial companies will be continuously reduced as privatization advances. At the end of each year, the State Ownership Fund was to make proposals for privatization of at least 10 per cent of the shares initially held, so the transfer of ownership would be completed within seven years. The sale of shares was to be done by the public offering of shares, by auctions which may be either open or limited to preselected bidders, or through direct negotiation. Shares could be sold preferentially to the employees and management staff who had the right to purchase up to a tenth of the shares offered for sale at a discount of 10 per cent below the public offering price.

Large scale privatization started in July 1992 with a public offering of shares in a state-owned Ursus brewery in Cluj. Privatization initially included 791 companies, representing all the industrial branches (27.3 per cent of them in textiles, 16.6 in engineering, 12.3 in wood processing, 11.8 in the chemical industry and 11.2 in electronics). But progress was slow and only 137 enterprises (17.3 per cent) were privatized by July 1994. These companies were very varied as regards the number of employees (between 45 and 9,473), but the textile (24.8 per cent), wood-processing (13.8) and food (10.7) industries predominated. The spatial distribution reflected local initiative, because the newly-privatized companies were mostly located in the smaller towns, but with clusters in Bucharest, Braşov, Oradea and Focşani.

In order to accelerate the process, a new programme was set up. Mass privatization was now to include 1,035 industrial companies (35.54 per cent of the total) employing 1,168.5 thousand people in all. It involved the distribution of nominal coupons which replaced the ownership certificates that had been largely sold below their value on the black market. Once again, the aim is to give equal chances to everybody. The law for the acceleration of the privatization process (Law 55 of 1995) called for a very tight schedule, with distribution of vouchers from August to September inclusive, selection of companies by voucher holders between October and December, and drawing up shareholder lists in respect of 30 per cent of the equity in the individual companies involved between January and March 1996. Once again enterprises were drawn from many branches: engineering, textiles, wood-processing, metallurgy and building materials. From the spatial point of view it is worth mentioning that the strongly industrialized counties were most prominent: selected enterprises accounted for 19.7 per cent of all industrial workers in Bucharest, 7.1 in Braşov, 5.5 in Prahova, 4.4 in Cluj, 4.3 in Argeş, 4.2 in Sibiu, 3.7 in Timiş and 3.1 in Mureş.

Some important issues, however, were clearly resolved. At the micro level, for example, the question arose of whether enterprises should be privatized in their entirety or only partially. There is a good case for the partial privatization of large or medium-sized enterprises in order to avoid unprofitable sales due to inexperience, under-valuation or unfavourable circumstances. At the macro level, should privatization apply to a complete industrial branch, or should there be a spatial perspective, selecting groups of interdependent enterprises from one region or another? The choice will affect the nature and intensity of inter-industry flows and the configuration of industrial specialization and co-operation relationships. The time scale for privatization may vary between large and small companies, for the preference given to employees of small enterprises to buy shares could delay the process according to their average salary available in 1992. Finally, should privatization be rapid or gradual?

Another long-standing dimension of privatization refers to the foreign capital investment. Unlike developed countries experiencing an exchange of investments based upon the reciprocity of transnational corporations, Eastern Europe is a large receiver of Western capital. Because of this one-sidedness the foreign investment law (Law 35 of 1991) gives guarantees and incentives to investors, as well as the unrestrained use of the profits earned by their activity. Imported machinery and equipment is exempt from import duties for a period of five years. Investments in industry are exempt from payment of profits tax for the period following the start of productive operations. Further concessions are granted if the profits are reinvested in enterprises set up in Romania, if half of the necessary raw materials, energy and fuels are imported or at least half the products and services are exported. Allowance is also made when expenditures are made for scientific research and for professional training; also when new jobs are created through new investment. In order to attract more investments, a new law was promulgated in July 1994 providing longer periods of exemption.

Apart from the favourable law framework, the Romanian economy is attractive for foreign investors because of the large size of the domestic market, sufficient to absorb new products or services especially when the demand is not already satisfied by the products available. Also there is the matter of accessibility to other markets, taking into account Romanian industry's traditional relations with the ex-Comecon countries as well as with others; and Romania's geographical position between the west and east of Europe and between Europe and the Near East: i.e. between different markets which could be complementary. The Danube and the Black Sea coast are significant for international and transcontinental communication; a cheap and skilled labour force is available following the decline of many of the state-owned enterprises; there are diverse natural resources, with more attractive potential than in many neighbouring countries; and Romania participates in international programmes initiated by the EU (e.g. 'Phare'), IMF and World Bank which contribute to the improvement of the economic infrastructure.

In total there are 41,670 joint ventures involving an investment of 1,268 billion US dollars. The most important investments have been made by South Korea, whose thirty joint ventures involve 156.8 million dollars, followed by the USA with an investment of 113.2 million dollars spread across 1,980 joint ventures. Germany is responsible for investing 111.9 million dollors (in 5,833 joint ventures); Italy 11.5 million dollars (in 4,650 joint ventures) and Great Britain 89.6 million dollars (in 586 joint ventures). Foreign investors have shown a preference for certain specific industrial branches: 26.8 per cent are in electronics, 16.2 in chemicals, 14.3 in engineering, 12.9 in the food industry and 12.0 in wood processing. Many of the joint ventures in chemicals and engineering are concerned with trade, consultancy and design. The two-thirds share of foreign investment comes mainly from Italy (20 per cent), France and Switzerland (12 per cent each), Germany (9 per cent) and the USA (8 per cent).

The spatial distribution of the joint ventures has two particular features: the concentration of about half the total number in Bucharest, mainly ventures in electronics, engineering and the chemical industry; and the location of the majority of joint ventures in specialized industrial centres having traditional export relations with foreign partners — hence the joint ventures set up at Berca and Boldeşti Scăeni (glass), Bistra (metallurgy), Bocşa (engineering), Fieni (electrotechnics), Oneşti and Mărâşeşti (chemical industry), Orăştie (textiles), Salonta (food industry) and Vascău (building materials). The inflow of foreign capital has made only a limited impact at the national level because the joint ventures tend to produce specific items for export. They are relatively isolated from the domestic industrial system.

Conclusions

The restructuring of Romanian industry is a matter of critical importance. Privatization is gaining momentum and foreign investment is increasing. Local and regional perspectives are important because of the scope for local initiative by the authorities and through the personal connections of Romanian managers, as well as through locational efficiency and industrial linkages in particular regions. Privatization in general, however, is complicated by its unprecedented scale and tight schedule timing, and also by the proliferation of institutions involved: the State Ownership Fund, Private Ownership Funds, the National Agency for Privatization and the Romanian Agency for Development, as well ministries, local authorities and prefectures whose responsibilities are not clearly specified. But the main reason for the slow pace of privatization in industry is the public's lack of confidence. The general economic decline (particularly the rapid decline in industrial output), rising unemployment and lack of interest in property rights after half a century of Communism depress public interest. Meanwhile there has been significant foreign investment, attracted by cheap but relatively highly skilled labour. Joint ventures are also developing according to industrial specialization and long-standing trade contacts. But it is essential that the joint ventures should act as cores of 'know-how' and information diffusion in order to stimulate other enterprises. There must be stronger convergence to link foreign investments with endogenous industrial development.

References

Ianoş, I. (1993), 'A Comparative Analysis between Urban and Industrial Hierarchies of Romanian towns in 1990', *GeoJournal*, 29, pp. 49–56.

Popescu, C. (1990), 'Tendinte actuale ale procesului de industrializare pe glob', *Terra*, 22 (1–4), pp. 57–61.

Popescu, C. (1991), 'L'impact du gigantisme industriel sur l'evolution des villes en Roumanie', *Revue Roumaine de Geographie*, 35, pp. 21–8.

Popescu, C. (1993), 'Romanian Industry in Transition', *GeoJournal*, 29, pp. 41–9.

Popescu, C. (1993a), 'Geographical Remarks on the Role of SMEs in Romanian Industry', *Revue Roumaine de Geographie*, 37, pp. 13–22.

Popescu, C. et al. (1988), 'Industrializarea si organizare spatiului geografic', *Terra*, 20 (3–4), pp. 67–75.

Popescu, C. et al. (1989), 'Diversificarea activitatilor industriale in centrele urbane specializate din Romania', *SSGGG Geogr*, 36, pp. 32–43.

8 Restructuring of Urban and Rural Settlement in Estonia

A. MARKSOO

Introduction

The transition from a centrally planned to a market economy involves crucial macroeconomic and social shifts in all the post-socialist states of Europe. These transitional changes have been especially great in the newly independent Baltic states, because in addition to the transformation of their economic and administrative systems they have also had to build up new state structures. All these changes have a fundamental influence on the spatial arrangement of their society, that is on their settlement system. It is the aim of this chapter to explain, taking the example of Estonia, to what extent the above-mentioned reforms, in their first five years of operation, have caused changes in patterns of urban and rural settlement. I also propose to diagnose very briefly possible trends in the near future.

This chapter is based mainly on data from the Statistical Office of Estonia (SOE). I have, however, had some difficulty in securing exactly comparable data due to the facts that (1) the new classification of statistics does not correspond exactly with the Soviet classification; and (2) the proportion of economic information processed by regions and individual towns is too small. For this reason, in places I have drawn on earlier research at the Geography Institute of Tartu University (carried out at the behest of planning institutions), and also on data collected directly from enterprises by students during their practical training in 1994. I refer to these sources below as the GI database.

The Estonian Settlement System at the End of the 1980s

Estonian settlement has a very long history; its network of towns, in the form of the older county centres, took shape essentially as early as in the thirteenth to the sixteenth centuries. Urbanization proper, however, began only in this century, reaching its climax in the decades following the Second World War, when Estonia was annexed by the former Soviet Union. While incorporated in that great power, the former agrarian-industrial economic structure of Estonia was rapidly replaced by an industrial structure. In the course of almost fifty years of Soviet power, Estonia was to traverse a phase of rapid extensive industrial development (1945–65), a stage of maturity (1965–80) and incipient stagnation (1980s). The latter was not expressed so much in diminished output as in the deterioration of economic indices and the ageing of technology. All of these development trends had their impact on the growth rate of urban and thus, indirectly, rural settlement (see Figures 8.1a and 8.1b).

When analysing the essence of the Soviet economic and ekistic policy and its influence on Estonian settlement one has to point out the following factors:

- all-round preference given to the growth of towns, so-called planned urbanization, which was also observed in all the Eastern and Central European countries (Musil, 1993);
- priority development of industry, especially stepping-up heavy industry. In Estonia special emphasis was laid on the industry producing fuel and electric energy to meet the needs of the St Petersburg (then Leningrad) area;
- military interests as a separate priority, numerous military bases and the special border regime. The latter seriously hampered the development and normal functioning of the smaller coastal towns and rural settlements; at the same time almost all foreign traffic was concentrated in the capital, Tallinn;
- continuous stimulation of immigration into Estonia in the interests of industry and national defence, as well as of long-term political aims;
- from the 1970s, centralization in the whole of economy, first and foremost in industry and agriculture, and continued consolidation of territorial concentration;
- distribution of state investments through the administrative hierarchy, which gave preference to the capital and the district (county) centres.

Owing to these, as well as to a number of other historical and geographical peculiarities, the Estonian settlement system was characterized in the pre-transitional period by the following features: Tallinn, the capital and the head of the system, overwhelmingly dominating the other towns; an incompletely developed group of second-rank towns, that is, regional centres with extensive hinterlands; a network of polyfunctional administrative county centres that had adapted themselves to the socio-economic potential of subordinated territory and had reached their ceiling; a large group of small towns markedly differentiated in their prospects and functions (local servicing centres, satellites, narrowly specialized industrial towns or seaside resorts);[1] and a network of central settlement (centres of large-scale farms, special servicing settlements, industrial townships, military settlements) still growing, versus the dwindling small villages in the rural areas.

The strong position of Tallinn among the other Estonian towns was, in the first place, due to its functions as capital. But Tallinn was also favoured and developed as a seaport, and an industrial and tourist centre of all-Union importance. As a result of such a two-sided development, Tallinn came to be the most multifunctional town in Estonia, becoming simultaneously the leading educational and scientific centre. At the same time, as the town expanded, two kinds of 'accusations' were raised against it. On the one hand, there were complaints that it did not leave room for the growth of other Estonian towns, and, on the other, it was pointed out that the local administration had lost control over its development. That sector in Tallinn's economy which was subordinated to all-Union ministries and was concerned with the harbour, the railway junction and the war industry existed as a 'state within a state', ignoring the republic's labour and migration policy (the attempts to switch over from extensive to intensive development), causing disproportions in the production and servicing sphere of the city. It was due to these facts that at the centre of the conceptions of development of Estonia's settlement at that time was the demand to restrict Tallinn's growth.

Estonia has only one real regional centre — the polyfunctional town of Tartu (the second most important educational, scientific and health services centre), whose sphere of influence extends over most of south-east Estonia. The other larger towns — Pärnu in the south-west, Narva and Kohtla-Järve in the north-east — do not equal Tartu, as far as their sphere of influence is concerned, and rank as third in the urban hierarchy. Pärnu is a polyfunctional town, but its growth and the spread of its influence was hampered in the Soviet period by restricted foreign maritime traffic, as well as by Tallinn's rivalry in western Estonia. The relations of Kohtla-Järve and Narva with their nearest hinterlands have been hampered by the peculiarities of their location (between the range of influence of Tallinn and St Petersburg on one side, and the Finnish Gulf and Lake Peipus on the other), as well as by their one-sided industrial structure and underdeveloped service and cultural sphere. As to their industrial output and the number of workers they exceeded both Tartu and Pärnu.

Despite Estonia's small territory and its limited population, the syndrome of core and periphery is clearly observable. In Estonia, the nature of fringe areas was expressed in the weakening of demographic potential (decrease and ageing of the population), in functional impoverishment, in a decrease in the abilities of self-management and in the impeded spread of innovations (Marksoo, 1992). It has not been possible to avoid the core–periphery syndrome in any country. In Estonia, too, this tendency was noticeable already before the Second World War, but during the past fifty years this development strengthened as a result of the capital's enforced growth and the closure of Estonia's western sea-border.

A concise survey of the demographic potential and the functional structure of Estonia's settlement system at the end of the 1980s is given in Figures 8.1a and 8.1b and Tables 8.1 and 8.2. Comparison of these tables shows what an essential role industrialization and the accompanying development of transport have played on immigration, and the difference in ethnic composition of Estonian towns. The role of the army was 'concealed' among other branches in the official statistics of the time.

Shifts in the Estonian Urban System

If we analyse the main developments of the transition period (retrieval of Estonian statehood and the restructuring of the economy, including privatization), it becomes clear that demographic processes, that is, people's reproductive, social and spatial behavior, have reacted to them quickest of all. The independence of Estonia and the withdrawal of Russian troops as a result thereof brought about a turn in external migration. While during the whole Soviet period in-migration from other parts of the Soviet Union was one of the main growth components of the Estonian urban population, now out-migration became one of the main reasons for the decrease of that population. The out-migrants are mostly non-Estonians and that brings about a small shift in favour of Estonians in the ethnic composition of the population. Towns still have a small migration loss in respect of the rural areas of Estonia. A turnaround in the rural–urban migration in favour of the rural areas took place in the first half of the eighties. At that time it was caused by the activities of large-scale farms who needed to recruit a young skilled labour force who were accorded various economic benefits. In the present transition period, the migration of the rural population to towns has been hindered by the unfinished land reform and the retarded retrieval of properties. Many country people are in a wait-and-see position. Besides, it is more complicated now to get a new abode and job. In addition to that, the new regulations of the migration statistics no longer prescribe the extraction from rural residence to town of young people leaving to study. At the same time it is probable that in 1992–93 the migration from town to country was to a certain extent fictitious. Since 1992, when the cost of heating in towns rose rapidly and the cost of central heating in houses was calculated per head, the subtraction of children and old people increased. Consequently, the real migration loss in the countryside should be smaller than reflected in official statistics.

Table 8.1 Estonian settlement system in 1989

Hierarchical stage	Rank size in 1,000s	Population (1,000s)	Estonians (%)	Non-Estonians (%)	% in industrial employment	% in Estonian industry (1988)
1 Capital[a] (Tallinn)	500	499.4	46.8	53.2	37	43.5
2 Regional centre (Tartu)	100–115	113.4	72.3	27.7	35	7.0
3 Polyfunctional centre: Pärnu[a]	50–55	56.9	72.4	27.6	39	3.6
Industrial agglomeration of NE Estonia	190–200	197.2	12.9	87.1	60	17.3
including Kohtla-Järve	70–80	77.3	20.9	79.1	56	8.7
Narva	70–80	81.2	3.9	96.1	53	8.2
4 County towns	5–25	144.2	80.1	19.9	10–38	8.9
5 Small towns	1–10	107.6	68.4	31.6	10-60	6.6
including with narrow specialization[b]	1–10	46.0	45.3	54.7	50–60	3.1
Total urban	—	1118.8	51.2	48.8	39	86.9
6 Local rural centres	1–2	29.9	86.3	13.4	—	—
7 Rural centres with narrow specialization	0.5–2	40.3	60.7	39.3	—	—
8 Farm centres	0.4–1	145.0	88.1	11.9	—	—
9 Other villages	0.01–0.4	231.7	91.3	8.7	—	—
Total rural	—	446.9	87.4	12.6	17	13.1
Total	—	1565.9	61.5	38.5	33	100

Notes

a with nearest satellites

b mainly industrial or transport centres; some of these towns are included in the agglomerations of Tallinn and North-East Estonia.

Sources: No. 4 in list of References at the end, and GI database.

Table 8.2 Ethnic aspect of the employment structure of Estonia in 1989

Activity	Total[a]	Urban population	Including Tallinn	Including other towns	Rural population
Total number of employed	850471	635770	290536	345234	214701
including % in:					
industry	33.1	38.6	37.6	39.4	16.9
construction	8.7	9.5	8.7	10.2	6.3
transport	7.2	8.6	10.0	7.3	3.2
agriculture and forestry	14.4	3.0	1.7	4.2	48.1
other activities	36.6	40.3	42.0	38.9	25.5
Total number of employed Estonians	495531	311844	129153	182691	183687
% share in:					
total employment	58.3	49.0	44.5	52.9	85.6
industry	45.0	40.0	37.4	42.0	79.3
construction	60.7	55.4	45.9	62.3	84.4
transport	46.4	42.5	31.9	54.6	77.5
agriculture and forestry	87.9	75.6	69.9	77.4	90.2
other activities	58.0	53.3	48.5	58.0	81.8

Notes

a The data of the census usually show the numbers of people in employment to be higher than the establishments' own labour accounts. According to the latter source, the average number of the employed population was 818,000 in 1989 (Eesti Statistika Aastaraamat 1990).

Source: Author's calculations based on data from the 1989 census from SOE.

Another prominent trend of the demographic processes in the transition period is the unprecedented fall in birth rates and a moderate rise in mortality (as a result of alcoholism, increasing casualties, crime and suicide), which is why natural loss begins to become a limiting factor for population growth. The decline in birth rates is mainly connected with the decline in the economy, partially also with the shift in young people's value system: they prefer a good career, business, travelling in the interests of creative activity or studies and so on, to having children. A conclusive survey of the dynamics of the urban population and its components is given in Table 8.3.

Table 8.3 Shifts in the dynamics of Estonian urban population

	Total change (1000s)	Natural gain or loss	Net migration	including: internal net migration	external net migration[b]
Total urban population:					
1989	8.0	4.7	3.3	-0.5	3.8
1990	1.9	2.4	-0.5	-1.5	1.0
1991	-2.7	-0.2	-2.5	-1.6	-0.9
1992	-35.7	-1.7	-34.0	-4.2	-29.5
1993	-18.8	-4.5	-14.3	-2.2	-12.1
1990–93	-55.0	4.0	-51.3	-9.8	-41.5
including:					
Tallinn[a]	-33.9	-3.1	-30.8	-8.4	-22.4
Tartu	-7.5	0.7	-8.2	-5.0	-3.2
Pärnu[a]	-0.7	-0.4	-0.3	0.7	-1.0
Agglomeration of NE Estonia	-8.8	-1.9	-6.9	0.5	-7.4
Kohtla-Järve	-4.7	-1.0	-3.7	-0.5	-3.2
Narva	-1.7	-0.4	-1.3	0.6	-1.9
County towns	-1.7	0.9	-2.6	1.0	-3.6
Small towns	-2.7	-0.2	-2.5	1.4	-3.9
with narrow specialization	-2.8	0.0	-2.8	0.6	-3.4

Notes

a With nearest satellites.

b The author has included in external migration also special migration, i.e. the movement of recruits and ex-service men. In the years 1990–92 hardly anyone joined the Soviet Army, but the number of those who returned after serving their time was considerable; this movement particularly reduced net out-migration. Later official SOE publications have not included special migration.

Source: Author's calculations based on data from SOE.

It appears that the population has diminished in all urban groups, both owing to migration (chiefly external migration) loss, and to natural loss. Tallinn has suffered the greatest absolute and relative decrease, having also a net out-migration in respect of the other Estonian towns and rural areas (at least according to official statistics). Data from the 1994 population statistics showed that natural loss was even greater (-5,671, including -2,650 in Tallinn and -1,556 in the North-East Estonian agglomeration), net out-migration, however, decreased: *c.* -9,100, including -6,900 external migrants (*Statistical Yearbook 1995*). In general, the decrease in the number of population has been greater in the towns where there are more non-Estonians and where there were more military personnel.

Connections between the decrease of population and employment and the growth of unemployment are not direct. The decrease in the number of people employed in the former huge textile mills, building-materials plants, cellulose and paper mills, machine-building and metal-working factories has been especially dramatic. Yet the period under discussion is rather short, with most of the unemployed having stayed on in their homes, hoping to find a new job, or they have sought employment in other fields of activity. The latter has been easier in the larger and polyfunctional towns. The unwillingness of the unemployed to move is observed also in several other European crisis areas (Millan, 1994). On the whole, changes in the number of urban population and its composition are relatively slight. The principal changes of the transition period, which could also be termed as shock shifts, appear, however, in employment, especially in its inner structure. The latter has several aspects, of which the most essential is the redistribution of workers between the formal and informal economies. By formal economy I mean the totality of established institutions that function within the accountancy system of state taxes and statistics. The informal economy has been given different definitions. U. Kockel (1992) distinguishes between two types of approaches here. Economists concentrate on the fiscal issues of tax evasion and unrecorded GDP, non-economists usually regard it as either an economic survival strategy, or a silent revolution heralding a better world, although both acknowledge that the informal economy spreads when the system has failed. In the case of Estonia, apparently both approaches hold true. Some enterprises, mostly the small and new ones, belong to the former type mentioned above, and make up the hidden sector of the economy in its narrower sense. The rest of the labour force is at present forced into the household and DIY economy, representing the so-called survival strategy. The majority of these people are trying to subsist on their vegetable plots and/or domestic animals, and occasionally also on various services (repairs, sewing clothes, and so on). It was estimated by the Ministry of Economy in Estonia that the informal economy accounted for *c.* 19 per cent of the total GDP in 1993. The amount of labour power employed in this way is impossible to determine from official statistical accounts. We can get some idea of it by looking at the following figures. In 1990 the average number of people employed in establishments and enterprises (including large-scale farms) was 710,400 (*Linnade ja maakondade...*, 1992). Not included in this figure are household workers, including farmers, freelancers and people employed by private persons, of whom there were few at that time. In 1993 the number of full-time wage-earning workers in the establishments and enterprises was 516,500; in addition, there were (at the end of the year) 31,560 contractual workers, part of whom are part-time workers (*Tööjõud ja pal Eesti Vabariigis*, 1994). Considering the fact that a part of the enterprises belonging to the formal economy do not give account of their labour force it is possible to estimate the approximate number of the people employed in this sector at 520,000, which totals nearly three-quarters of the 1990 level. To ascertain the amount of labour power engaged in the informal economy we have to take into account the decrease in the total number of workers as a result of migration (*c*. 25,000), and the number of unemployed. Owing to the fact that unemployment benefit is very small in Estonia, and the procedure for securing it requires breaking bureaucratic barriers, the official level of unemployment appears to be very low: it was below 2 per cent of the working-age population in 1993. The number of the people on the dole varied from 21,300 to 14,700 in the course of the year. According to EMOR (the Estonian counterpart of Gallup), actual unemployment was 8–9 per cent (Kuddo, 1994) among those of working age, thus *c*. 65,000 people. On the whole, it appears that Estonia has at least 150,000 people deriving their income from the informal economy (in its larger sense), taken together with the unemployed, who have to do odd jobs because of the low level of unemployment benefits. Another bigger shift is in the workers' redistribution between the primary, secondary and tertiary spheres (Table 8.4 overleaf).

Table 8.4 shows that the decrease in the overall number of workers has been replaced by a slight increase, mainly at the expense of the tertiary sphere. At the same time, the outflow of workers from the primary sphere, especially from agriculture, goes on unchecked.

In analysing the employment structure by the different groups of urban settlements we are again confined to estimates. The collection of data brought out a certain regularity: the larger the town, the more imperfect its statistics, and vice versa. Therefore the data on employment in the larger towns (except in Tartu) in Table 8.5 are barely approximate; data on the county centres (five towns) are somewhat more reliable; and those on the small towns (twelve) are fairly exact. By the rate of restructuring of activities I mean the rate of alteration in the three basic spheres of activities; by the new activities I mean mainly educational institutions, banking and insurance agencies of a new type, furthering international economic ties and cultural contacts, various counselling centres, real estate agencies and info-agencies.

Table 8.4 Estonia: redistribution of employees in basic spheres of activity (formal economy)

Year	Average number of full-time workers	including % in: primary sphere[a]	secondary sphere	tertiary sphere
1990	710400	24.9[b]	36.7	38.4
1993	516520	13.9	33.0	53.1
1995 (1st quarter)	535591[c]	9.9	34.3	55.8

Notes

a Also includes mining.
b Workers at large-scale agricultural and fishing farms together with servicing personel.
c Calculated by 95 per cent confidence interval.
Sources: Nos. 13, 20 and 21 in list of References at the end.

Table 8.5 shows that in the larger, polyfunctional towns the transition has proceeded more smoothly than in the narrowly specialized and smaller ones. The decrease in employment has been estimated on the basis of the number of workers in the enterprises of any given town, and the unemployment rate on the basis of the population of working age in the same town. As compared to the decrease in the number of jobs, unemployment in small towns is relatively low for two reasons. First, among the dismissed workers there were a fairly large number of residents from the surrounding rural areas not included in the unemployment figures for the towns. Secondly, several small towns are situated close to the capital or some other larger towns, which is why people who have lost their jobs in them have started to commute to work in the larger towns. Innovations have mostly reached the first and second rank towns, Tallinn and Tartu, where the contraction of industry has been compensated for by expanded international functions. This is especially true of Tallinn, which now belongs to the second level of the Middle and Eastern European capitals, the so-called B-category centres (together with Riga, Vilnius, Bratislava and Ljubljana). In the same hierarchy, Tartu belongs to the C-category centres, mainly thanks to the international relations of its university and its research institutes (*Zentrensysteme als Träger*, 1994).

Table 8.5 Changes in the employment and functional structure of Estonian urban settlements (1990–94)

Hierarchical rank	% decrease in formal employment 1990 = 100	including in industry	% unemployment 1.01.1994[c]	Rate of restructuring of activities[d]	Foundation of new activities[d]
1 Capital	15	35	0.2	xxx	xxx
2 Tartu	22	37	1.4	xx	xx
3 Pärnu	25	40	1.4	xx	xx
Kohtla-Järve	30	35	4.5	x	x
Narva	30	35	6.6	x	x
4 County towns[a]	28	32	2.7	xx or x	x
5 Small towns[b]	32	37	3.0	x	x

Notes

a Generalization is made on the basis of five towns.
b The same for 12 towns.
c Persons receiving unemployment benefits, as a percentage of the working-age population (reflects about a quarter of real unemployment).
d xxx = strong, highly active; xx = medium; x = weak.
Source: GI Data-base and no. 13 in list of References at the end.

On the Changes in Rural Settlement

Changes in rural settlement are, first and foremost, caused by land reform and changes in the forms of enterprise in agriculture. The privatization of agricultural enterprises, which constitute the main sphere of activity in the rural areas, and their adjustment to the market economy has proceeded along two parallel lines: restoration of privately owned farms, on the one hand, and formation of larger units — joint-stock companies and co-operative societies — on the basis of the former large-scale farms, on the other. The agricultural reform was begun at the end of 1988, when the privately owned farm law was adopted and the parcelling out of the large-scale farms became an urgent problem. The most characteristic feature of the initial stage of the reform, from 1989 to the middle of 1991, was the creation of new privately owned farmsteads, the basic structure of the large-scale farms remaining practically unchanged. In the course of this two-and-a-half-year period, over 7,000 private farms were officially registered at the county level, albeit many of them small: what might be called hobby-farms, capable of providing the owner with an additional income. Most of these farmers went on working on the large-scale farms or continued as state officials. The second stage of the agricultural reform began in the second half of 1991. With the adoption of the ownership law and the land law there emerged the principle of restoration of illegally alienated property to its lawful owners and the broadening of the circle of inheritors. As a result, the restitution of land became considerably more complicated, and the formation of private farms was slowed down, a certain revival coming only at the end of 1993. The situation has also aggravated by the deepening of the economic depression and changes in the government's agrarian policy (prices, the crediting system, the policy of foreign trade, and so on) (Table 8.6).

Table 8.6 Dynamics of the private farms in Estonia

Number of farms January 1 (by region)[a]	1991	1992	1993	1994	Land per farm (ha, 1994) Total	Arable	Share of farms (%) of total arable land
NW Estonia	2228	2223	2029	3379	26.7	11.1	9.0
NE Estonia	296	296	252	341	25.0	7.2	5.6
SE Estonia	3141	3066	2733	4472	22.4	11.1	11.3
SW Estonia	1145	1130	962	1634	27.1	11.2	9.0
W Estonian Islands	218	216	404	326	27.3	7.0	3.2
Total	7029	6924	6380	10152	24.9	10.9	9.8

Notes

a NW Estonia includes counties: Harju, Lääne, Rapla, Järva, Lääne-Viru; NE Estonia: Ida-Viru; SE Estonia: Jõgeva, Tartu, Põlva, Võru, Valga; SW Estonia: Viljandi, Pärnu; W Estonian Islands: Saare, Hiiu.

Source: Author's calculations on the basis of nos. 2, 7 and 13 in list of References at the end.

Table 8.6 shows that the role of private farms in Estonian agriculture is very small so far, especially in north-east Estonia and on the islands. Many farms are still in the making: by 1 January 1994, only one fifth (1,946 farms) had had ownership of their land confirmed (*Eesti maakatastri aastaraamat*, 1994). In the second stage of reform, mainly during 1993, an overwhelming majority of the rural areas brought to an end the reorganization of the large-scale farms, which has in fact consisted in cutting them into smaller units, mostly joint-stock companies and co-operative societies. The majority of them have specialized in complex agricultural produce, others only in some kind of livestock farming. Usually the farm machinery repair shops, saw-mills and other auxiliary plants split off as small independent joint-stock companies. As a result of the reorganization of large-scale farms, many different productive enterprises have come into being, but at the same time the number of jobs in them has decreased considerably. Many new enterprises proved to be economically weak owing to the incompetence or self-interest of the reorganizers and have by now gone bankrupt. The general atmosphere of encouragement of privatization and entrepreneurship has brought about quite a boom in the countryside, as well as in towns, primarily in the sphere of servicing and catering. New shops, bars, restaurants, as well as places for tourists, such as motels, camping sites and tourist farms crop up everywhere. The development of servicing, however, has failed to add massively to the number of jobs, because most of the enterprises are small. Some of the places set up in 1992–93 soon closed down.

Setting out to find out what impact the reforms have had on the dynamics of rural population and their employment, one has to point out that during the 1980s the demographic situation in the Estonian countryside improved. As a result of the turnaround in rural–urban migration and the increase in birth rates, the rural population began to grow slowly and its age composition rejuvenated. Over the period 1981–89, the total rural population grew by slightly less than 9,000 (438,000 in 1981 and 446,800 in 1989), but the number of 0–15-year-old children grew by 9,600 and that of 16–29-year-olds by 12,800. The number of pensioners, however, decreased (by 11,600). The demographic situation also improved in the majority of fringe communes. But during the transition period, owing to diverse economic difficulties and especially because of the loss of the feeling of security, the birth rate has again abruptly fallen and natural gain has been replaced by loss (1990–93: -1,600). The external net migration, largely due to the departing Russian military and their families, has been negative (1990–93: -8,300), while the internal net migration, on account of urban settlements, has been positive (+9,800). I would like to emphasize once again that the gain is in fact smaller, because large numbers of young people who have moved to towns to acquire their education have not been counted as migrants. Hence, the total permanent rural population has been relatively stable (444,800 as of 1 January 1994). So far there is no great change in the age composition of the rural population, including in fringe areas. On 1 January 1994, the 0–15-year-olds made up 25 per cent, those of working age (men aged 16–54, women aged 16–55) made up 52.3 per cent, and those of pensionable age 22.1 per cent (*Eesti valdade...*, 1994). Among the urban population the corresponding figures were 21.4, 57.0 and 21.6 per cent respectively.

As in the case of the urban population, the greatest shifts in rural population are dependent on the employment structure (Table 8.7).

Table 8.7 Estonia: changes in employment structure of rural population

Region	Year (1 Jan.)	Total no. of employees	including: hired workers	farmers[a]	entrepreneurs & individual workers	employees in auxiliary households	Work-age population not working or studying[b] number / % of total	including officially unemployed number / % of working age
NW Estonia	1989	95445	94418	—	157	870	—	—
	1995	74428	62876	4115	3281	4156	15112	1644
	+/-	-21017	31542	4115	3124	3286	15.2	1.6
NE Estonia	1989	11958	11834	—	31	93	—	—
	1995	8312	7297	358	114	543	2301	901
	+/-	-3646	-4537	358	83	450	19.4	7.6
SE Estonia	1989	64100	62487	—	162	1451	—	—
	1995	50501	39093	4636	1544	5228	14444	3224
	+/-	-13599	23394	4636	1382	3777	19.7	4.4
SW Estonia	1989	31852	31195	—	58	599	—	—
	1995	26931	21465	1633	901	2932	5497	955
	+/-	-4921	-9730	1633	843	2333	15.0	2.3
W Estonian islands	1989	14503	14340	—	19	144	—	—
	1995	12393	10093	848	443	1184	2603	755
	+/	-2110	-4247	848	414	1040	15.5	4.5
Total	1989	217858	214274	—	427	3157	—	—
	1995	172565	140824	11415	6283	14043	39957	7379
	+/-	-45293	73452	11415	5856	10886	16.8	3.1

Notes

a In 1989 the number of private farmers was very small and was taken to belong to the group of entrepreneurs.

b This group does not include invalids and mothers who take care of 0–3-year-old children.

Source: Author's calculations on the basis of nos. 4 and 9 in the list of References at the end.

In the period 1989–94, the overall employment rate had fallen by one fifth, and the number of wage-earners by about one third. In 1994 the numbers of the employed population stabilized, mainly on account of the individual workers and employees in auxiliary households. The number of hired workers decreased as before, but at a slower rate. They still make up the prevailing majority (four-fifths) of the total number of employed people. Formally, the decrease in the employment rate in the countryside is no greater than in the towns. But the overwhelming majority of the rural wage-workers are employed in agricultural co-operative societies and joint-stock companies, where the wages are extremely low. In the first quarter of 1995 the average wage in Estonia was EEK 2,086; in agriculture it was barely EEK 1,173 — that is, the lowest among all the other spheres of activities (*Wages and Salaries*, 1995). Most of the farmers, too, exist on the subsistence level. It should be pointed out here that in the mid-1980s workers in agriculture earned on average more than industrial workers. Thus, the fall in living standards makes itself felt more acutely in the countryside than in the towns.

The above changes in the employment of the rural population also presuppose changes in the location of jobs, which should be reflected in the redistribution of the population between different types of settlements (Table 8.8 overleaf).

From the given figures it becomes evident that the total rural population has decreased in north Estonia largely at the expense of the narrowly specialized centres, which have lost part of their population for two reasons: first, because of the emptying of military settlements, and secondly because of a decrease in the numbers of inmates in the institutions (hospitals, homes for invalids and orphans) located in these settlements. The farm centres, formerly the main growth centres among rural settlements, have suffered losses in their population mainly since 1992, when the number of jobs was abruptly reduced in the reorganized large-scale farms. This is also characteristic of the county of Harju, the nearest hinterland of Tallinn, the capital, where the farm centres continued to grow rapidly up to 1993.

Table 8.8 Estonia: dynamics of rural population by patterns of settlements in 1989–94[a]

		Population				
		Total	Local centres	Narrowly specialized centres	Farm centres	Other villages
1/1/1989		446941	29914	403184	145046	23166
31/1/1995		440784	29716	30909	139760	240399
+/-		-6157	-198	-9409	-5839	9289
the same by regions:						
NW Estonia	1995	178818	17557	16443	60955	83863
	+/-	-7460	-65	-8432	-2818	3855
incl. county of Harju	1995	71117	9668	6788	26318	28343
	+/-	-7758	-71	-8878	464	727
NE Estonia	1995	22311	3262	1792	7658	9599
	+/-	-1782	-603	-162	-1222	205
SE Estonia	1995	139853	4347	8994	40949	85563
	+/-	1044	237	-502	-459	1768
SW Estonia	1995	68316	1944	2055	23985	40332
	+/-	688	78	-466	-439	1515
West Estonian islands	1995	31486	2606	1625	6213	21042
	+/-	1353	155	153	-901	1946

Notes

a Population numbers by rural settlements are given on the basis of accounts of the rural communes on their households. These accounts do not contain data on military men or prisoners in some rural places.

Source: Author's calculations based on nos. 3 and 9 in list of References at the end, and GI Data-base.

As the population of the central settlements has decreased, the number of inhabitants in the other villages has gone up in all counties without exception. This is partly a result of the creation of private farms, but also a sign of the growth of that part of the population who have lost their jobs and are trying to avoid the expensive flats in farm centres and to secure their livelihood on their own small auxiliary households (a small plot of land with a few animals). As for the latter, conditions are often better in smaller villages.

Hence, one can observe a certain trend towards deconcentration and simultaneous population redistribution in Estonia's rural areas. Yet these shifts are still small and essentially have not diminished the regional differences in the extent of concentration in rural settlements (Table 8.9). In heavily urbanized north-west and north-east Estonia, rural settlement shows greater concentration, too. Many of the central settlements here are also satellites of the neighbouring towns.

Table 8.9 Estonia: extent of concentration in rural settlement in 1995

	Average population in			Share in total rural population (%)	
	farm centres	narrowly specialized centres	local centres	all central settlements	including farm centres
NW Estonia	592	783	1951	53.1	34.1
incl. county of Harju	1012	754	1934	60.1	37.0
NE Estonia	547	597	1631	57.0	34.3
SE Estonia	431	818	869	38.8	29.3
SW Estonia	470	685	972	41.0	35.1
West Estonian islands	311	542	1303	33.2	19.7
Total	494	754	1486	45.2	31.7

Source: Author's calculations based on no. 9 in list of References below, and GI database.

Conclusion

Although the transition period has been brief and therefore the economic and political reforms are still half-way through, they have made themselves felt both in urban and rural settlement. The overall trend has been towards a drop in demographic potential with simultaneous deconcentration of settlement. The latter is expressed, first and foremost, in the slowing down in the population growth of the capital, the larger industrial centres and the central settlements in rural areas. The above-mentioned changes characterize only the first stage of the transition period, in many respects a state of shock, where the main thing is to stay alive, to survive the hardships. The impact of economic factors has manifested itself mainly locally, in the fall in birth rates, the rise of mortality in settlements and in the decline of employment. The changes in the spatial mobility of the population, first of all the turnaround in external migration (re-migration to Russia), have chiefly been caused by political factors. Economic 'levers' have not yet begun the redistribution of population in Estonia. Up to now there is even a certain contradiction between the migration streams and the concentration of the economic potential. So Tallinn is predominantly concentrating new enterprise and attracting foreign investments, but its population has decreased. In the countryside the fall in living standards and levels of production has been the greatest, but population figures have mostly been stable.

It is highly probable that in the next few years this inertia in population mobility will disappear and economic factors will play a leading role in determining migration trends. No doubt it is most important how the rural population will behave. If no supporting measures are taken in agriculture (so far they do not exist), the number of bankrupt farms and collective farms will soon increase abruptly and people will begin to stream to the towns. Therefore it is very important to decide how much agricultural production Estonia needs and what measures are necessary to guarantee it. The development of the whole settlement system in Estonia depends on this.

Taking into consideration the already perceivable trends, i.e. the internationalization, tertiarization and de-industrialization of the economy and (hopefully) the moderate contraction of agriculture, the development scenario of settlement in Estonia might be as follows:

- Tallinn begins to grow again and its leading role among other towns will increase even more, therefore the dilemma will persist: is it possible and necessary to limit the growth of Tallinn to save resources for other towns, or not?
- Tartu, as the second town, will preserve its position and strengthen it a little, not so much on account of its growth but due to the diminishing share of the industrial agglomeration of north-east Estonia.
- The population in the north-east Estonian agglomeration will evidently decrease as in-migration from Russia has stopped, and after its reorganization and modernization industry here needs less labour. Thus the outflow from here would continue: re-migration to Russia, as well as migration to other parts of Estonia, especially Tallinn. There is no great probability that the Estonian authorities' attempt to resettle more Estonians in north-east Estonia will give noticeable results.
- The county towns would, generally, retain their position in the Estonian urban system as far as their size and traditional functions are concerned. At present the west Estonian centres which are also sea resorts and more open to foreign contacts have more favourable

conditions for innovations. The county towns in east Estonia are suffering now because they have lost ties with the Russian market.

- It is inevitable that differentiation is still more pronounced in small towns and rural central settlements: some of them are regressing because they are not able to find their bearings after losing their former functions (bankruptcy of a big plant, disintegration of a large-scale farm) and hesitate to make a new start in new branches of activities; others have preserved a stable basis of further development or are working to establish it.
- The preservation of small villages and dispersed settlement in the countryside now depends on the success of the regional policy that is being introduced.

Note

1 In the Soviet period the so-called local functions also included co-operation with the neighbouring collective and state farms (also called large-scale farms) that had often built their offices and dwelling houses in small towns or in close proximity to them, thus making a contribution to the development of their social infrastructure.

References

1 *Eesti maakatastri aastaraamat 1993*, Tallinn, 1994, p. 79.
2 *Eesti Statistika aastaraamat 1990*, Tallinn, 1991, p. 445.
3 *Eesti Vabariigi külanõukogude ja maa-asulate rahvastik 1970.a., 1979.a. ja 1989.a. rahvaloenduste andmeil*, Tallinn, 1990, p. 168.
4 *Eesti Vabariigi maakondade, linnade ja alevite rahvastik 1989, I*, Tallinn 1990, p. 158.
5 *Eesti Vabariigi maakondade, linnade ja alevite rahvastik 1989, III*, Tallinn, 1991, p. 72.
6 *Eesti Vabariigi maakondade, linnade ja alevite tööjõuressursid 1989. Statistiline kogumik*, ESA, Tallinn, 1990, p. 59.
7 *Eesti valdade rahvastik valdade majapidamisarvestuste andmetel seisuga 1. jaanuar 1993*, Tallinn, 1993, p. 70.
8 *Eesti valdade rahvastik valdade majapidamisarvestuste andmetel seisuga 1. jaanuar 1994*, Tallinn, 1994, p. 145.
9 *Eesti valdade rahvastik valdade majapidamisarvestuste andmetel seisuga 1. jaanuar 1995*, Tallinn, 1995, p. 141.
10 *Estonian Statistics 1993*, nos. 1 and 7.
11 Kockel, U. (1992), 'Provisory Economy and Regional Development: Towards a Conceptual Integration of Informal Activities', in M. Tykkyläinen (ed.), *Development Issues and Strategies in the New Europe*, Newcastle upon Tyne, 1992, pp. 101–19.
12 Kuddo, A. (1993), 'Estonian Labour Market', *Eesti Pank Quarterly Review*, 1993, no. 4, pp. 19–37.

13 *Linnade ja maakondade sotsiaal-majanduslik seisund 1991. Statistika kogumik*, Tallinn, 1992, p. 155.
14 *Linnade ja maakondade sotsiaal-majanduslik seisund 1992. Statistika kogumik*, Tallinn, 1993, p. 170.
15 Marksoo, A. (1992), 'On the Role of Urban Centres of Fringe Areas in Estonia', in M. Tykkyläinen (ed.), *Development Issues and Strategies in the New Europe*, Avebury, Newcastle upon Tyne, pp. 163–9.
16 Millan, B. (1994), 'Europe 2000: Territorial Aspects of European Integration', *Eureg*, 1994, no. 1, pp. 3–8.
17 Mysil, J. (1993), 'Changing Urban Systems in Post-Communist Societies in Central Europe: Analysis and Prediction', *Urban Studies*, vol. 30, no. 6, pp. 899–905.
18 *Statistical Yearbook 1995*, Tallinn, 1995, p. 282.
19 *Zentrensysteme als Träger der Raumentwicklung in Mittel- und Osteuropa*, Projektleiter: F.-D. Grimm, Beiträge zur Regionalen Geographie, Institut für Länderkunde, Leipzig, 1994, p. 156.
20 *Tööjõud ja palk Eesti Vabariigis. 1993.a. 1. osa*, Tallinn, 1994, p. 142.
21 *Wages and Salaries 1/95*, Statistical Office of Estonia, Tallinn, 1995, p. 75.

Figure 8.1a Urban system of Estonia: hierarchical-functional structure

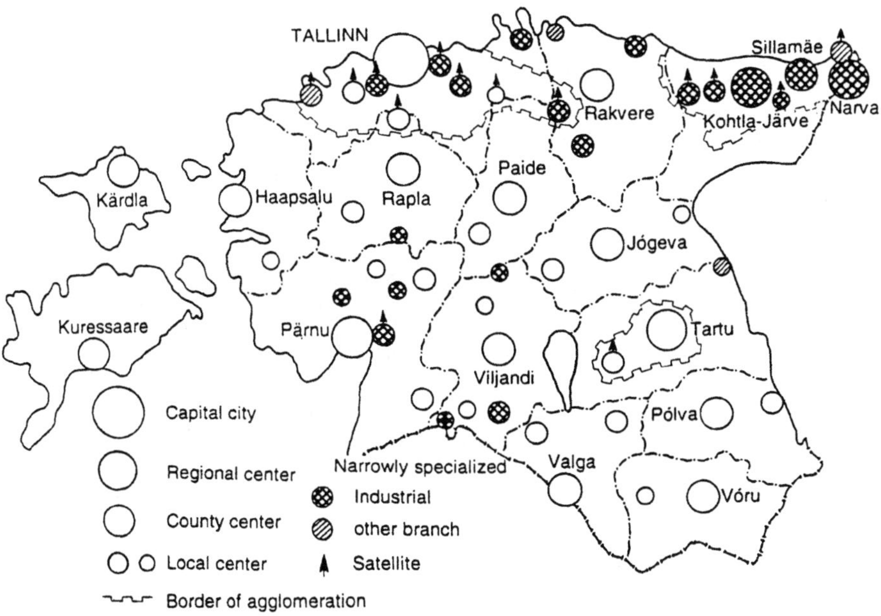

Figure 8.1b Urban system of Estonia: core and periphery

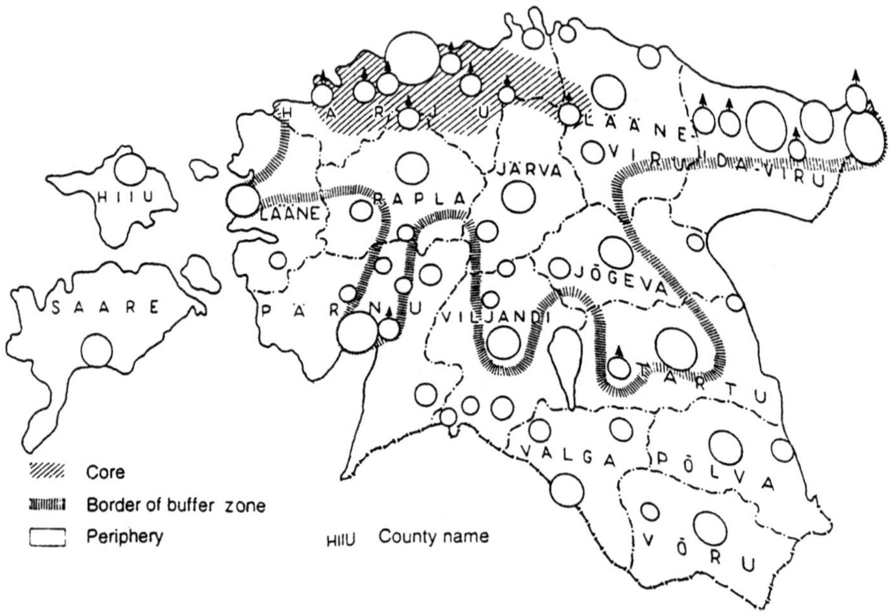

9 The Transformation of Polish Retailing

ANDRZEJ WERWICKI

Among all branches of the Polish economy, the earliest, deepest and most advanced changes have been those in the distribution system. This has been the result of two factors: legal and infrastructural. Owing to these changes, the number of shops rose from 125,000 in 1988 to 385,000 in 1993, while the total number of all (retail) points of sale rose from 227,000 in 1988 to 630,000 in 1991 and to 780,000 in 1993. The scarce number of private retailing enterprises in 1988 (43,000) had risen, by the end of 1990, to 346,000, while the number of state-owned retailing units dropped from 183,000 to 123,000. By 1993, 97.7 per cent of all shops were in private ownership.

Legal Aspects of the Transformation

The foundation for the privatization process in the distribution system was a series of parliamentary bills passed at the beginning of 1990. Of special importance were: (1) amendments to the bill on economic activity to allow free enterprise; (2) the privatization bill covering state-owned enterprises; and (3) the bill abolishing the government monopoly on foreign and wholesale trade. Also of great importance was the law on premises, which liberated rent-fixing. These new legal principles, introducing total freedom of commercial activity, although at times giving rise to certain abnormalities, generally freed foreign trade from currency regulations and set in motion new distribution channels by way of which, in a market used to permanent shortages of consumer goods, there appeared, in almost unlimited quantities, rare products practically unknown in state socialist retailing.

Infrastructural Aspects of the Transformation

Among the infrastructural regulators of the transformation process, a basic part was played by the stock of existing shop premises and the levels of rent charged for them. This stock of shop premises consisted of three basic types:

(1) normal shop premises actually used by the state socialist retail system;

(2) permanent kiosks functioning as shops in localities with a deficit of regular shop premises (mostly in peripheral districts of intensively developing urban areas, as well as in villages); and

(3) old, mostly unused as such since 1950, small shop premises then being used as dwellings.

State-run retail shops were usually large, especially in fast-growing cities, as well as in localities badly damaged during the Second World War and therefore cleansed of their smaller shop premises. The new freedom in rent levels often resulted in their being over-valued, which in the initial period of transition often made them difficult to privatize. Of the existing 124,000 shop premises in 1989, until the second half of 1991 only 31 per cent had been taken over by private retailers. Most of these were in western Poland, where in some voivodships the percentage of private shops exceeded (or came close to) 50 per cent of the total (Katowice, Łódź, Zielona Góra and Jelenia Góra, Koszalin, Legnica, Opole, Wrocław). Sometimes, too, privatization was hampered by uncertainty over the property rights of the premises.

The sudden rise in registered private retailing enterprises should also be linked with the re-use for retailing purposes of old small premises previously used as dwellings. This was the case in numerous small towns and larger villages all over the country. All this appeared to be insufficient, however, to redistribute the increasing amount of goods which began to be imported. From the beginning of 1990, the main streets of cities began to witness pedlars and hawkers offering various goods for sale from primitive stands and even boxes. As time passed, they gradually built kiosks and other types of semi-permanent selling arrangements along main urban shopping streets. Along Marszałkowska Street in Warsaw, for example, in February 1991 there existed 500 such selling points. At the same time there was a resurgence in the tradition of local markets, which in the previous decades had ceased to function. Such markets appeared all over the country. Some eventually became huge bazaars of international repute, especially among the 'commercial tourists' coming from beyond the eastern border. In Warsaw, one such market first appeared right in the middle of the city centre, in Parade Square in front of the Palace of Culture. In the middle of 1991 it had about 1,200 selling units. The city authorities, elsewhere as well as in Warsaw, began to set these markets in order, which resulted in the formation of neatly arranged bazaars, usually located outside city centres. Until the end of 1993 they still showed signs of development, although their flourishing period is now behind them. This regulation of the bazaars gave rise to companies and administrators responsible for hygiene and maintaining order, and also for collecting stall rents from the traders, which were later partially handed on to the local authorities. Generally, retailing is the main function of the bazaars in question, although there is an exception in a group of big wholesale markets south of Łódź, in the proximity of Tuszyn and Rzgów, where a large share of the products sold is manufactured in small private industrial enterprises producing clothes, textiles and knitted goods.

To close this discussion of the organizational forms of private retailing in Poland, I should mention so-called mobile retailing. This type of commercial activity is characteristic not only of rural areas, but to a large extent also of the big bazaars, where mobile retailing is an important element. The mobile retailing enterprises are registered in the owners' place of residence, not in the area of their activity.

In comparing the now permanently functioning retail establishments with those existing in Poland up to 1989, it is impossible not to observe that, apart from the huge extention in their number and variety and the quality of the goods offered, the private retailers have made impressive progress in equipping their shops and in their attentiveness to interior design and layout, as well as in displaying the goods on sale. In this respect the transformation of Polish retailing is most advanced. Most Polish shops now do not differ greatly from those in Western Europe. The most visible remaining difference is in the quality of the service.

According to the latest data on Polish retailing, at the end of 1993 one point of sale occured per forty-nine inhabitants, with one shop per 101 inhabitants (compared to one shop per 168 inhabitants in 1985). Most numerous were general food stores and butchers' shops (altogether forming 35.9 per cent), and their number was constantly growing. Also numerous were clothes shops (8.7 per cent) and those selling leather goods and footwear (4.0 per cent).

Although these figures show people's increasing access to retailing outlets, this access was enjoyed only by a small proportion of the population. Large retailing enterprises were few in number and located only in the traditional main shopping centres of larger cities. In the biggest of them, such as Warsaw, Cracow, Łódź and Poznań, one might already observe the appearance of a few large foreign retail outlets, dealing in high quality and luxury consumer goods.

In 1949, the Communist government began its so-called 'battle for socialist retailing', as a result of which private retailing was almost eliminated from the market, leaving only small outlets dealing in craftsmen's and food products. That said, however, in the Eastern Bloc only East Germany enjoyed private retailing more widespread than in Poland; in the remaining countries of the Eastern Bloc private retailing was almost non-existent. The years 1989–91 may be described as the 'second battle for retailing', this time aimed towards its privatization. The main thrust of this battle has almost been completed: co-operative and public-sector outlets now form probably less than a quarter of all retail establishments. The task facing Polish retailers in the near future is to adjust to existing (and changing) demand, which may be reflected in the ever-increasing branching and diversification of the Polish retail system.

References

Werwicki, A. (1992), 'Retailing in Poland', International Journal of Retail and Distribution Management, vol. 20, no. 6, pp. 34–8.

Werwicki, A. (1994), 'Transformacja sieci handlu i usług na obszarach przygranicznych Polski w latach 1989–1992' (Transformation of the Retailing and Service Networks in Polish Border Regions), Podstawy rozwoju zachodnich i wschodnich obszarów przygranicznych Polski, Biul. no. 5, pp. 151–61.

10 The Process of Socio-Economic Change in East-Central Europe after 1989: A View from Western Europe

ANDREW H. DAWSON

> There is a tide in the affairs of men which, taken at the flood, leads on to victory. — Shakespeare, *Julius Caesar*, IV, iii.
>
> He who hesitates is lost. — Proverb.

In his welcome to the conference at which this chapter was presented, the *wojewoda* of Toruń expressed the hope that its proceedings would help forward the process of socio-economic transformation which has been occurring in Central and Eastern Europe since 1989. It is in that spirit that the following comments are offered upon the two chapters (both presented at the conference) about the changes that have taken place in Poland: 'Transformations and Dilemmas of the Polish Economy' by Chojnicki, Czyż and Parysek, and 'The Transformation of Polish Retailing' by Werwicki.

The chapter by Chojnicki et al. describes the reforms which have been pursued and the effects they have had upon both the sectoral and regional structure of the Polish economy. It points to some of the malign consequences of the changes, hints that the continuing apparent economic weakness of some of the more backward voivodships is a measure of the fact that there will inevitably be much more change to come before the effects of forty years of central planning have been purged from the economy, and concludes that a new and vigorous regional policy is required before the country's current problems can be solved. Werwicki's chapter outlines the revolutionary expansion which has occurred in the retail sector since the legalization of private enterprise and commerce. In other words, the implications of the two chapters would seem to be in direct conflict. Whereas the first seems to suggest that the transformation of Poland to a market economy has become so problem-ridden that the completion of the process may no longer be acceptable to the population and can only be achieved by some new strengthening of the planning machinery, Werwicki's chapter chronicles a story of rapid, and largely problem-free, adaptation to the stimulus of the free market.

I wish to comment in four ways upon this apparent conflict of interpretation. First, there is, of course, no certainty about the outcome of the process of reform. It may lead to the establishment of a thriving, market-based economy, enjoying widespread support among Poles. Alternatively, the problems of high and rising prices, crime, unemployment and the persistence of regional disparities, which Chojnicki et al. have associated with it, may become so serious that the electorate will react even more strongly than it did at the 1993 election — when it voted for a breathing space in the pace of reform — and return instead to the former policies of state intervention. It should be noted, however, that Poland has already made very substantial progress in its programme to shrink the role of the state; and that, following the privatization which has already occurred, less than half of the economy remains in the hands of government — a situation which is not very different from that of most of the so-called market economies in Western Europe. It should also be noted that, notwithstanding the shocks which it suffered in the early 1990s, by 1993 Poland had achieved one of the fastest rates of economic growth in Europe — a rate which it has managed to retain since. It may also be relevant to recall that, while unemployment in Poland has risen sharply to a rather high level, that level is considerably lower than that which has existed in Spain for several years. In the aftermath of the Second World War, the Polish people made a prodigious effort to rebuild their country, and there is no reason to believe that, if they wish to make the less traumatic changes in their way of life which were announced by the Mazowiecki/Balcerowicz government in 1990, they cannot do it.

Whether they wish to continue on the road to reform may well depend, however, upon the extent to which the changes accompanying it are perceived to be fair. It is already clear that there has been a great widening in the range of personal wealth in the country since 1989, with not only the emergence of some very rich people but also the appearance of beggars; it was already the case that, in some parts of the country, registered unemployment in 1993 and 1994 encompassed more than a quarter of the workforce; and it has been freely admitted by the Polish authorities that they have experienced considerable difficulty in balancing the budget, in large part because of problems in the collection of taxes from some of those in the private sector. In short, the early outcome of reform would seem to have been anything but equitable. My second comment would be to suggest that fairness in this situation might be achieved in part through a more imaginative use of taxation. Following the reforms of the early 1990s, turnover tax has ceased to be the predominant source of government revenue — though it will remain important until the privatization of the remaining large state-owned enterprises has occurred — for it has been supplemented by taxes on profits, employment (in the form of social insurance payments), incomes and consumption. It is doubtful that this shift, though necessary, has been in the right direction: taxes on profits inevitably reduce the resources which are available for new investment, those on labour discourage employers from taking on workers, and many who should be paying such taxes seem to be evading them. Nevertheless, the present taxes do contain some elements which could provide a basis for imposts which would both be difficult to evade and would remove the economic rents which are accruing to those who have found themselves in a position to exploit the opportunities created by the rapidly changing Polish space economy. During the 1980s, taxes were imposed on private-sector farmers, taxes which were related to the price of one of the country's staple cereal crops, the quality of land and the area of farms. They were set at a low level, and took no account of the returns which were available to farmers who produce speciality crops, either in areas which enjoy a favourable climate, such as the fruit-growers in Nowy Sa_cz, or those who are close to large urban markets, such as the vegetable-growers around Warsaw and in Upper Silesia. They could, however, be increased, not least to take account of the fact that farmers are now enjoying the opportunities which a largely unregulated, and indeed somewhat protected, market affords. Secondly, the rapid expansion of the retail sector, and its concentration in the centre of Warsaw — beginning with the unregulated sale of goods on the streets — after 1989, was followed by the imposition of charges by the authorities for the use of such sites. Those charges do not, however, seem to have discouraged the expansion of retailing that has occurred, and there may, therefore, be scope for raising them further. Moreover, the principle of removing the economic rents which accrue to the users of land in cities might be extended to others who have profited from changes in the markets for housing and office space. It also follows that a switch from taxes on investment and employment to one on rents would be likely to bring the incidence of taxation into line with that of economic success and failure among voivodships which has been identified by Chojnicki et al., taxing those regions into which foreign investment is flowing and in which unemployment is low — which were identified in their chapter as being 'strong' — more heavily than those which are 'weak'. The economic geography of Poland would probably become very different if such a system of taxation were to be introduced: it is likely, however, that it would be perceived to be much fairer.

It is never likely, however, to be a geography in which all parts of the country enjoy an equality of success, for free markets, by their nature, not only seek out the opportunities which the varying characteristics of site and situation offer for the pursuit of profit from place to place, but are also continuously creating such spatial diversity. Thus, free markets oblige capital and labour to migrate to places in which they can earn more than at present, while threatening those who are unwilling to move or otherwise adapt their economic activities with bankruptcy. It follows that, at any moment, there will be regions of capital accumulation and inward migration, which will be more prosperous, and others, from which capital and labour are withdrawing, which will be less so. It is also the case that any activity by government which inhibits or discourages these types of adjustment or which leads those involved to believe that they can be protected from such change runs the risk of reducing the dynamic of the market and the welfare to which it gives rise, as well as imposing on the producers of wealth the direct costs which are involved in such regulation. The decision by Poland to embark upon a programme of reform, and to adopt the market rather than central planning as its model for future economic management, is, I would suggest, a one-way street; and thus my third comment would be to draw attention to the fact that the conclusion by Chojnicki et al. — that the contrasts which have appeared between the 'strong' and 'weak' voivodships are now so great that they require the creation of some new element of regional intervention to deal with them — would appear to be at best a hesitation in the programme which the country has adopted, and at worst a call for its reversal.

Lastly, it is unfortunate that these two chapters have paid such little attention to Poland's international economic links. Any medium-sized economy is obliged to be relatively open if it is to keep up with the pace of innovation in the rest of the world; and the reforms since 1989 have had as one of their principal elements the need to replace the barriers endemic in the system of central planning by a new freedom to trade. Furthermore, all the countries of Central and Eastern Europe have expressed a wish to become more closely associated with the European Union, and some, including Poland, are eager to join that Union as soon as possible. It has, therefore, been a matter of embarrassment to many within the Union that, after forty years of preaching about the superiority of market economics, their governments should have sanctioned an Association Agreement which gives Poland only very limited access to Western European markets, and that those governments should now be dragging their heels over the prospect of full Polish membership. What is more, although the European Union conference in 1996 debated the future enlargement of the Union and offered

Poland full membership of the Union early next century, it may not be able to extend support at anywhere near the same level in respect of either the Common Agricultural Policy or the Cohesion Fund as it has done to other recent entrants. Such a situation does offer Poland the opportunity to examine the alternatives which are available to it, one of which would be to exploit its location 'at the heart of Europe' by renewing its traditional links with Eastern Europe and, in particular, Russia. The formation of a free trade zone, which might also encompass Belarus and Ukraine, would not only open up the opportunities which inevitably exist for trade between neighbours, but perhaps also revive Poland's late-nineteenth-century role as a pivot between the capital exporters of Western Europe and the markets of the East. Following the imposition of steep tariffs on the import of goods into the Russian Empire at that time, Western Europeans established factories not only in St Petersburg and Moscow, but also on a large scale in Òoådzå, Sosnowiec and Warsaw — the nearest places to them which lay within the tariff wall — a process which could happen again if Poland, a stable country close to Western Europe but with long-established links with Russia, were to turn itself into an entrance to the eastern half of the continent. Such a policy reversal might, moreover, have other effects. An overture to the East would challenge the European Union to decide whether or not it is willing to accept Poland as an equal partner; and, in offsetting fears of Russian isolation in the new Europe, might do much to undermine the xenophobia which has been growing in that country. In short, this is a tide which Poland is uniquely well placed to take.

11 Environmental Geopolitics and Shock-Shift Transition in the Czech Republic

ANDREW TICKLE

Introduction

The analysis of the post-1989 transition in Central and Eastern Europe, from 'real existing' socialism to new forms of polity, is an area ripe with opportunities for interdisciplinary social science — and geographers in particular (Michalak and Gibb, 1992; Dostál and Hampl, 1994a, pp. 229–30). Whilst human geographers have traditionally focused on spatial patterns of social phenomena (agriculture, housing, industry and so on), more recent theoretical interpretations emphasize the structure of society which reproduces such relations. Similarly, our understanding of the 'environment' or 'nature' has moved on from utilitarian analyses of natural resources to wider concepts based on notions of socially produced 'nature'. Thus, just as 'Western' social theorists are acknowledging the role of environmental issues in late modern society (Beck 1986, 1988; Beck et al., 1995), I would argue that spatial aspects of societal transformation in Eastern Europe are also closely bound up with what some term 'green' issues, or as I have termed it — 'environmental geopolitics' (*sensu* Kára, 1992).

The chapter by Hampl and Müller in this volume recognizes the importance of 'society in its environment' and tends towards a regulationist interpretation of transition whereby the 'transformation processes necessarily result in changes of geographical organization'. Hampl and Müller also suggest implicitly that modes of enterprise regulation (and hence patterns of uneven development) are contingent primarily on economic and political factors, although they acknowledge that 'ecological and technical barriers' to development may emerge in later periods of the transformation.

This echoes earlier work which suggests that the transition from totalitarian society to a new trajectory of democracy (interpreted as 'plural democracy and a market-driven economy') will be constrained by various institutional and organizational factors (Dostál and Hampl, 1994b, p. 193). In the rest of this chapter, I hope to show that the 'environmental factor' is not solely a secondary, late or post-transition issue but has interacted significantly, both institutionally and organi-zationally, in the transition and in important pre-figuring processes.

In addition, there is a clear spatial dimension to environmental issues and policies — from the international to the local — that strongly overlaps with the space-economy, thus affecting development (investment) choices. This is explored in the third section but needs first to be grounded through a brief consideration of relevant theoretical and methodological issues.

Theoretical Considerations

A number of contemporary studies are now beginning to address some of the key geographical issues associated with transformation processes in the Czech Republic (for example, Dostál et al., 1992; Pavlínek, 1992; Barlow et al., 1994). For Slovakia a series of regulationist approaches have shown the transition — thus far — to be a highly uneven process (Smith, 1994, 1995, 1996), a conclusion also indicated by Hampl and Müller.

A number of methodological truisms stand out from such approaches which are worth re-emphasizing. For example, traditional approaches to location theory tend to emphasize economic factors at the expense of 'contingent historical relationships' (Smith, 1989, p. 142). Put more simply, in trying to understand new and future patterns of development, we must look partly to the past, in this case former state socialist planning in Czechoslovakia.

This regime of capital accumulation and regulation was highly extensive and aimed at reducing regional unevenness, particularly through the use of forced 'socialist industrialization'.[1] As much of this development (both industrialization and urbanization) took place in the Slovak space-economy (Hamilton, 1971; Smith, 1994), the Czech Republic suffered concomitantly, mostly in the Prague and Brno hinterlands (Dostál and Hampl, 1994b). Within this 'development' process, however, little regard was paid to environmental constraints in locational choice, beyond that of basic utilization of the surrounding milieu for sources of raw material or sinks of waste products.

It is also implied by the term 'shock-shift' that the nature of the transition is radical and the process highly dynamic.[2] This means that the complexity of change will often defeat meaningful analysis, especially when limited or 'snapshot' data are used. Thus current analyses of geographical differentiation in the Czech Republic (see, for example, Table 3.1 in Hampl and Müller's chapter) may mean little without reference to a time-series dynamic. Many of the key transformational indicators they use, however (for example, numbers of entrepreneurs, joint venture companies and so on), are entirely novel economic features not currently amenable to long-term trend analysis.

In addition, the unique nature of the transformation from a centrally planned to a mixed/market economy creates formidable difficulties in relating any empirical or theoretically-based interpretations of change to the diverse body of extant geographical theory on the spatial distribution of development. Indeed, some contend that 'Western' political geography (in particular 'state-centred' and 'world-systems' frameworks) will inevitably fail to meet the theoretical challenge posed by the downfall of Communist systems (Michalak and Gibb, 1992).

Finally, given the speed of change, it certainly seems premature to theorize a smooth transition to known 'Western' capitalist economic models. Limited empirical evidence gathered thus far would suggest that this is far from being the case for Slovakia, and that other, possibly intermediary, modes of regulation are currently emerging (Smith, 1994, 1996).

Environmental Factors Affecting Societal Transformation

As many studies have indicated, both for Communist systems in general (for example, Pryde, 1972; DeBardeleben, 1985; Carter and Turnock, 1996) and for the former Czechoslovakia in particular (Vavroušek, 1990; Moldan, 1990), environmental constraints generally had a marginal influence on economic development and industrialization. In the case of Czechoslovakia, this was not for lack of laws, policies or rhetoric emanating from the central state apparatus. For most enterprises and managers, however, the fulfilment of planned targets took priority over environmental controls, leading to intensive, though often localized,,industrial pollution.

This highly visible failure of Czechoslovak state socialism to protect the environment, combined with Marxist-Leninist rhetoric that environmental problems only occurred as a result of capitalist modes of production, gave rise to questions of regime legitimacy. This in turn led to the environment being used as one of the primary forms of oppositional protest in state–society discourse (Tickle and Vavroušek, 1996). Thus ecological opposition can be seen to prefigure the popular protests that formed the backbone of the Czechoslovak 'velvet revolution' of November 1989.

Conversely, strongly pro-environmental rhetoric was a significant legitimating feature of the post-1989 political landscape, echoed by both the newly democratic parties and government alike.[3] The new constitutional arrangements also meant that the environment became one of a number of crucial issues that would still be dealt with on a federal level — a significant institutional and organizational commitment which would potentially challenge and constrain some political and economic objectives.

This is not to say that previous state environmental policy had no effect on socio-economic development; for example, international commitments made in 1985 in the United Nations Economic Commission for Europe's Convention on Long Range Transboundary Air Pollution (UN ECE CLRTAP) to curb sulphur dioxide (SO_2) emissions (from fossil-fuel burning) gave rise to a new geography of energy production with an emphasis on nuclear capacity sited in predominantly rural southern and eastern locations, as opposed to the concentration of brown coal-burning power stations located in the traditional industrial areas of North Bohemia and the Moravia–Silesia borders. This pro-nuclear policy has been continued post-1989, even though SO_2 emissions have fallen significantly (37.1 per cent from 1980–93: Elvingson, 1995) due to industrial decline rather than new nuclear plant coming on-line. Current commitments to other global environmental treaties on ozone depletion, carbon dioxide emissions and biodiversity are also likely to act as constraints across key industrial (especially energy production) and agricultural sectors.

More generally, and in the context of the modern Czech Republic, the environment has been cited as being influential in the space-economy for a number of reasons (Kára, 1992, pp. 187–8). First, variations in the quality of the environment affect location decisions, both nationally and internationally: low quality regions are unlikely to attract inward investment. In addition, variation in environmental standards can be a factor in locational choice — either positively (in environmental terms) by promoting harmonization and higher standards (as the Czech Republic has generally done in relation to European Union [EU] norms: Cole, 1995) or negatively by lowering standards and encouraging 'dirty' investments, for example, trade in toxic waste (Kruszewska, 1993; Manser, 1993, pp. 14–15).

Thus in Smith's model of globalized enterprise regulation (Smith, 1995, pp. 771–2) the stringency of environmental standards promoted by the state may be a key variable in attracting foreign direct investment (FDI). At present, however, although many of the former socialist states have improved environmental standards, this must be seen against powerful forces of deregulation, both in the European (EU-dominated) and global economy (for example, the recently agreed Uruguay Round of the Global Agreement on Tariffs and Trade, GATT).

Lastly, environmental perceptions vary strongly between nations and this has given rise to notable problems for both the Czech and Slovak Republics, especially in their relationship with Austria and Hungary over a number of energy-related issues. The most long running tension has been the construction of the Gabčíkovo hydroelectric dams system on the Danube (Dunaj) between Hungary and Slovakia. Although the scheme is now working (and generating significant amounts of electricity for Slovakia), the course of the project has been strongly influenced by environmental factors, especially in Hungary (Galambos, 1993). Similarly, Austrian ecological pressure (both from government sources and environmental groups) has been influential in nuclear energy policy and may, in relation to the Mochovce nuclear power plant project, have caused serious damage to Slovakia's perceived reliability as a partner for foreign investment and aid (Williams, 1995).

Looking at wider, regional effects on the space economy, the role of the European Union (EU) is potentially of much greater significance. The EU has a specific aim of helping Central and Eastern Europe towards democracy and market economies (for a variety of reasons, including trade potential, military security, an expanded power base and so on), and a strategic part of this reform package is said to be aimed at environmental aid and co-operation (Baker, 1995). This occurs partially through the Phare[4] programme which instead appears to have acted as a 'trojan horse' for FDI assistance — at the expense of environmental and other projects (Gowan, 1995).

A similar charge can be made against the other significant transitional aid institution for Eastern Europe — the European Bank for Reconstruction and Development (EBRD) — which has generally failed to live up to its founding ideal to provide a new 'Marshall Plan' for Eastern Europe, especially in the field of environmental reconstruction (Manser, 1993, pp. 153–5). Much of its environmental aid has focused on nuclear safety investment in conjunction with Western nuclear interests (both state and private). In the recent linked case of Slovakia's nuclear plants at Jaslovské Bohunice and Mochovce, however, the EBRD has been forced to reconsider its loan package by some of its member states on environmental grounds.

Thus the role of the environment in EU involvement in the economic transition has been, in general, rather less positive than might be anticipated from the original policy rhetoric of 1989 and 1990. Indeed, in some areas it may be anticipated that EU involvement could actually be detrimental both to the environment and to regional economic development. This is particularly the case in relation to the development of European transport infrastructures.

The EU, in common with many authorities, believes that the development of road networks is a pre-requisite to economic well-being. This is echoed by Czech views which also suggest that enhanced infrastructural links into the West European economic space could facilitate political integration (Musil, 1994, p. 169). A number of concerns stand out. First, it is far from clear that such an alteration of spatial relationships will address the implicit problem of uneven development in the East European region. As with the well-known example of the Appalachians in the 1960s (Smith, 1989, p. 144), such enhanced geographical links — without addressing concomitant socio-economic issues — may reinforce current unevenness by allowing migration to more prosperous centres and regions, possibly beyond the Czech Republic.

This latter view is reinforced by suggestions that in building the 'missing links' (north–south and east–west through Eastern Europe) in the trans-European road network, much reliance will be put upon 'transit' motorways which, with tolls and limited connections to local networks, may be of limited benefit to the recipient country. Finally, it should also be added that road building and the increased road traffic that follows have serious environmental impacts *per se*, but despite this current Phare funding is heavily skewed against rail investment.

Thus it is argued that environmental issues such as these, plus many others not outlined above (for example, contaminated land liability; land restitution involving protected areas such as National Parks, nature reserves and so on; local protests over waste dumps, incinerators, nuclear storage repositories and so on) do place certain 'constraints' (spatial, sociological, political and economic) on the pace and direction of economic transition, particularly where decision-making is shared with other countries or supra-national institutions. Given the conflicts that some of these issues have generated, this suggests that environmental dimensions need to be better integrated into future models of state and society in Eastern Europe. The possibilities for this are addressed below.

Concluding Remarks

The environmental problematique is already well embedded in the societal and political landscape of the Czech Republic, mostly thanks to the despoiling effects of the former Communist regime and the environmental protest movement it engendered. Further legitimacy was given to the topic by its institutional prominence during the initial political transition (1990–92). Since then, however, popular support has waned as other social problems (wages, cost of living, unemployment, crime and so on) have come to the fore. In addition, the hegemonic influence of neo-liberal economic theorists, both in government and from global institutions such as the World Bank, has seriously marginalized attempts to integrate environmental factors into economic planning.

This is due to the belief that a swift transition to a free market economy (shock-shift) is the sole guarantor of stable democracy and economic growth and, as such, has undeniable primacy over 'secondary' issues such as the environment. Also implicit in this reasoning lies the assumption that capitalist, market-centred models of development will promote environmental quality *per se*. On a global scale, however, this is a questionable assumption, as most environmental indicators still show disturbing downward trends, especially in the less-developed 'south'. The rhetoric of 'free market' economics also fails to take on board the issue of *sustainable* economic development — a concept that is now broadly accepted as the main guiding principle in national and global environmental governance. The concept has also been transmuted into the term 'sustainable restructuring' to specially describe the aim of restructuring Central and East European economies such that 'it does not adversely affect the ecological system' (Manser, 1993, p. 149).

Manser (ibid.) cogently argues that whilst investment in environmental protection was increased initially in many countries (see also Balcerowicz, 1995, p. 333), insufficient strategic control (that is, a virtually 'hands-off', *laissez-faire* approach), especially with regard to Western investment, meant that the opportunity for 'leap-frogging' environmental problems inherent in Western economic models and implementing a pro-active, precautionary approach (*de novo*) had been lost. Much of the blame for this can be laid at the door of Western governments and allied interests (particularly multinational companies), who have generally failed to look beyond their own narrow self-interest in the global reproduction of their economic fiefdoms.

But returning to a potential research agenda for geographers, what does this mean in spatial terms, or more specifically for the Czech and other East and Central European space economies? Currently, environmental resources and quality are not evenly distributed and this is part of the emerging geographical unevenness in the region that others describe (Hampl and Müller, this volume; Smith, 1996). On an international scale, concern has also been expressed that East–West environmental quality may *diverge* further (Kára, 1992), a worrying possibility hinted at by a number of trends suggested above ('dumping' of Western pollution in the East; lack of substantial economic/environmental aid; trade tariffs and so on).

Hampl and Müller also conclude that differentiation tendencies are likely to increase in the future (allied to possible ecological and technical limits) and tantalizingly suggest that certain 'compensation' processes (unfortunately unspecified) may operate against such effects in the most affected areas ('exposed agglomerations'). For them, a final key question is how might *appropriate* levels of unevenness become 'self-regulating'. Leaving aside the desirability of such an endpoint, answers to this question will diverge strongly according to the future polity envisaged.

The current Czech government bases its governance on the reductionist rationality of economic solutions imported from Western models of development, and this may be harmful to both democracy (Wheaton and Kavan, 1992, p. 185) and the development of regional well-being, both economic and environmental. This would suggest that the 'transition to capitalism' will not necessarily provide the simple and benign evolutionary succession that has been characterized by some observers (Michalak and Gibb, 1992).

Instead, paraphrasing Smith (1996), the value of 'counterhegemonic alternatives for pathways out of the collapse of state socialism' needs to be recognized, especially if the transition is to move towards any notion of regional sustainable restructuring. To effect this will require a rupture in current environmental geopolitics that will be contingent on wider political pluralism, both in terms of a greater state tolerance of civic initiatives in the Czech Republic and the international ability of diverse social movements to challenge the global enterprise culture.

Acknowledgements

I would like to thank Frank Carter and Professor Maik for their initial invitation to Toruń and the School of Geography and Environmental Management, Middlesex University for providing my travel costs. David Smallbone (Middlesex University), Adrian Smith (Sussex Univerity) and Ian Welsh (Cardiff University) all kindly commented on drafts of the paper. Needless to say, they bear no responsibility for the final text.

Notes

1 See Hamilton (1971) for a useful historical overview of socialist planning and its effect on industrial location.
2 The word 'shock' appears to derive from the term 'shock therapy', the neo-liberal economic treatment advocated by Sachs (1990) for the economies of the East European region.
3 For example President Havel's 1990 New Year address and Marian Čalfa's 'state of the nation' speech to the joint federal assemblies on 27 February 1990 (*East European Reporter*, vol. 4, no. 1, pp. 56–8 and vol. 4, no. 2, pp. 8–10, respectively).

4 'Poland, Hungary: Assistance for Restructuring Economies'. Since 1990 this was widened to include Bulgaria, Czechoslovakia, Yugoslavia and East Germany, and in 1991 Albania and the Baltic states were included.

References

Baker, S. (1995), 'EU Environmental Policy in East and Central Europe: The Role of the European Union', in A. Blowers and P. Glasbergen (eds), *Environmental Policy in an Internaioal Cotext*, London.

Balcerowicz, L. (1995), *Socialism, Capitalism, Transition*, Budapest.

Barlow, M., Dostál, P. and Hampl, M. (eds) (1994), *Territory, Society and Administration: The Czech Republic and the Industrial Region of Liberec*, Amsterdam.

Beck, U. (1986), *Risikogesellschaft: Auf dem Weg in eine andere Moderne*, Frankfurt am Main (translated as *Risk Society: Towards a New Modernity*, London, 1992).

Beck, U. (1988), *Gegengifte: Die Organisierte Unverantwortlichkeit*, Frankfurt am Main (translated as *Ecological Politics in an Age of Risk*, Oxford, 1995).

Beck, U., Giddens, A. and Lash, S. (1995), *Reflexive Modernization: Politics, Tradition and Aesthetics in the Modern Social Order*, Oxford.

Carter, F. W. and Turnock, D. (1996), *Environmental Problems in Eastern Europe*, 2nd edn, London.

Cole, J. (1995), 'European Union Air Protection Legislation: Is the Czech Republic Ready?', *European Environment*, vol. 5, no. 5, pp. 145–9.

DeBardeleben, J. (1985), *The Environment and Marxism-Leninism*, Boulder, CO.

Dostál, P., Illner, M., Kára, J. and Barlow, M. (eds) (1992), *Changing Territorial Administration in Czechoslovakia: International Viewpoints*, Amsterdam.

Dostál, P. and Hampl, M. (1994a), 'Conclusions: Further Research Directions', in M. Barlow, P. Dostál and M. Hampl (eds), *Territory, Society and Administration: The Czech Republic and the Industrial Region of Liberec*, Amsterdam.

Dostál, P. and Hampl, M. (1994b), 'Development of an Urban System: General Conception and Specific Features in the Czech Republic', in M. Barlow, P. Dostál and M. Hampl (eds), *Territory, Society and Administration. The Czech Republic and the Industrial Region of Liberec*, Amsterdam.

Elvingson, P. (1995), 'ECE Convention: Extent of Compliance with the Protocols', *Acid News*, no. 5, December.

Galambos, J. (1993), 'An International Environmental Conflict on the Danube: The Gabčíkovo-Nagymáros Dams', in A. Vari and P. Tamas (eds), *Environment and Democratic Transition: Policy and Politics in Central and Eastern Europe*, Dordrecht.

Gowan, P. (1995), 'Neo-Liberal Theory and Practice for Eastern Europe', *New Left Review*, no. 213, pp. 3–60.

Hamilton, F. E. I. (1971), 'The Location of Industry in East-Central and Southeast Europe', in G. W. Hoffman (ed.), *Eastern Europe: Essays in Geographical Problems*, London.

Kára, J. (1992), 'Gepolitics and the Environment: The Case of Central Europe', *Environmental Politics*, vol. 1, no. 2, pp. 186–95.

Kruszewska, I. (1993), *Open Borders, Broken Promises. Privatisation and Foreign Investment: Protecting the Environment through Contractual Clauses*, Greenpeace International, Amsterdam.

Manser, R. (1993), *Squandered Dividend*, London.

Michalak, W. Z. and Gibb, R. A. (1992), 'Political Geography and Eastern Europe', *Area*, vol. 24, no. 4, pp. 341–9.
Moldan, B. (ed.) (1990), *Životní prostředí České republiky* (Environment of the Czech Republic), Prague.
Musil, J. (1994), 'Development of Prague: Long Term Trends and Scenarios', in M. Barlow, P. Dostál and M. Hampl (eds), *Development and Administration of Prague*, Amsterdam.
Pavlínek, P. (1992), 'Regional Transformation in Czechoslovakia: Towards a Market Economy', *Tijdschrift voor Economische en Sociale Geografie*, vol. 83, no. 5, pp. 361–71.
Pryde, P. R. (1972), *Conservation in the Soviet Union*, Cambridge.
Sachs, J. (1990), 'What Is to Be Done?', *Economist*, 13 January.
Smith, N. (1989), 'Uneven Development and Location Theory: Towards a Synthesis', in vol. 1 of R. Peet and N. Thrift (eds), *New Models in Geography: The Political-Economy Perspective*, 2 vols, London.
Smith, A. (1994), 'Uneven Developments and the Restructuring of the Armaments Industry in Slovakia', *Trans Inst Br Geogr NS*, vol. 19, pp. 404–24.
Smith, A. (1995), 'Regulation Theory, Strategies of Enterprise Regulation and the Political Economy of Regional Economic Restructuring in Central and Eastern Europe: The Case of Slovakia', *Regional Studies*, vol. 29, no. 8.
Smith, A. (1996), 'From Convergence to Fragmentation: Uneven Regional Development, Industrial Restructuring, and the 'Transition to Capitalism' in Slovakia', *Environment and Planning A*, vol. 28, no. 1, pp. 15–56.
Tickle, A. and Vavroušek, J. (1996), 'Environmental Politics in the Former Czechoslovakia', in A. Tickle and I. Welsh (eds), *Environment and Society in Transition: Central and Eastern Europe*, Harlow.
Vavroušek, J. (1990), *Životní prostředí a sebeřízen' společnosti* (The Environment and the Self-Management of Society), Prague.
Wheaton, B. and Kavan, Z. (1992), *The Velvet Revolution: Czechoslovkia, 1988–1991*. Boulder, CO.
Williams, K. (1995), 'The Foreign Relations of Independent Slovakia', *Slovo*, vol. 8, no. 2, pp. 87–108.

12 The Prospects for Slovenia: Some Opportunities and Constraints

JOHN SARGENT

Introduction

In the foregoing chapters, Professors Klemenčić and Sanguin have provided us with valuable and objective accounts of current trends in Slovenia, Klemenčić offering a survey of the economic geography of his country in its physical and historical context, and Sanguin an analysis of the geography of Slovenia's ethnic minorities. In what follows, my comments are not so much aimed at a critical discussion of the contents of the two chapters, but instead attempt to focus on two interrelated issues arising from the chapters: identification of domestic opportunities for economic growth in Slovenia, and tensions (some of which stand in the way of accelerated growth) between Slovenia and her neighbours.

Opportunities for Growth

In his introduction, Klemenčić draws our attention to the advantages enjoyed by Slovenia in its drive towards faster economic growth. Two of these — namely size of territory and environmental diversity — perhaps deserve further emphasis. Slovenia is clearly fortunate as regards the size and compactness of its territory: it is easier to develop a modern, efficient infrastructure in a country the size of Slovenia than in a country the size of Poland; compactness of territory is no doubt more permissive of all kinds of integration economies (for example) than is great extent of territory.

One other feature, advantageous in the quest for accelerated economic growth, sets Slovenia apart from most of the other countries of Eastern Europe. There is in Slovenia, perhaps mercifully, relatively little in the way of old-fashioned and polluting heavy industries. Metal-bashing, energy-hungry, smoke-stack manufacturing industry exists — witness the steel works at Jesenice — but far more representative of Slovenian manufacturing are industries such as textiles, electrical engineering and pharmaceuticals. From this, *inter alia*, two results follow: Slovenia has emerged from Communist rule without serious or large-scale instances of industry-induced environmental catastrophe; and the burden of industrial restructuring (with its attendant problems of reallocation of labour) is not as onerous in Slovenia as it is in many of the other former socialist states of Eastern Europe.

Slovenia possesses many other advantages. Klemenčić hints at peculiarities in the ownership of industry in former Yugoslavia, where factories were ownded not by the state, nor by individuals, but by the factory workers, a practice known as 'social ownership'. This system caused problems during the first two years of independence (that is, 1991–92), for example when a major foreign investment (the purchase of equity in Tobacco Company Ljubljana by the Franco-German firm Reemstmap-Seita) was delayed by uncertainty over the legal procedures for purchasing property that was held under social ownership;[1] but this drawback has been largely overcome, and has in any case been greatly outweighed by the tradition of flexible and autonomous factory management established in the days when Slovenia was a component republic of Yugoslavia.

Most Slovenian factories — a higher proportion than elsewhere in Eastern Europe, one suspects — are run by small- and medium-scale enterprises (SMEs). It is difficult to find recent data purely for the manufacturing sector, but in 1992, some 92 per cent of all firms in Slovenia employed fewer than fifty workers.[2] Many of Slovenia's small factories are operated by people who also engage in farming; and many of them produce goods for export. Many of Slovenia's small factories are located in the countryside (hence the close link between small-scale manufacturing and agriculture), their rural location being made possible by the presence of an unusually well-developed infrastructure, including, in this small and compact country, a dense road network.

Very similar patterns of small-scale manufacturing (linked to part-time farming) exist in East Asia, most notably in Japan and Taiwan. The role of manufacturing SMEs in the modernization of Japan has long since been recognized by Japanese and Western scholars — indeed this is a topic that has attracted a substantial body of scholarly research.[3] During the period of Japanese colonial rule, Taiwan (like Slovenia a compact territory) became equipped with a well-developed infrastructure, including a good network of rural roads. This provided the basis for the rise of small industrial enterprises in the countryside — small factories that have not only helped to produce a geographically even pattern of wealth throughout the island, but have also played an important part in the whole of Taiwan's modern economic growth.[4]

But one need not range as far afield as East Asia to find examples of the way in which small business can contribute to economic success. On Slovenia's western doorstep, in the plains of Friuli, there exists a landscape in which prosperous farms alternate with many small factories. Though Lombardy and Veneto probably offer more vivid and more numerous examples of dynamic small-scale manufacturing, the immediate hinterlands of Pordenone and Udine provide ample support for the proposition that small business has contributed powerfully to the post-1960s rise in Italian living standards.[5]

Whether in Italy, Japan or Taiwan, small manufactuing businesses can make the following beneficial contributions to economic growth: unlike large firms, they are generally quick and flexible in responding to changes in the market; they are often breeding grounds for entrepreneurial talent; when linked to farming, they can survive economic fluctuations (their workers can retreat into agriculture during economic downturns and return to manufacturing when growth is resumed); and, when located in the countryside, they can act as an important brake on rural depopulation — they can play a useful role in dampening regional variations in living standards. And as the Italian and Japanese examples readily show, small firms can be surprisingly adventurous, whether in adopting advanced technology, or penetrating export markets.

Slovenia is fortunate to possess an unusually large number of small manufacturing businesses, many of which, as already noted, are located in the countryside. The expansion of SMEs is, of course, quite inadequate on its own as a prescription for accelerated economic growth. And, one has to admit, the extent to which European SMEs can compete with their counterparts in China and South-East Asia is very limited — competition with low-cost producers in East Asia is an issue that confronts manufacturers in both Eastern and Western Europe. The Italian and Japanese experiences, meanwhile, suggest that the promotion of SMEs is far from being the best way of enhancing state revenue. But these qualifications apart, SMEs can play a most valuable role. Their potential in Slovenia (and for that matter elsewhere in Eastern Europe) should not be underestimated.

Problems Ahead

It is easy to be optimistic about the future of Slovenia, and indeed the temptation is strengthened by the frequent portrayal of the country as an autonomous Alpine state more akin in character to Austria and Germany than to the Balkans.[6] (This imagery overlooks the fact that a high proportion of southern Slovenia is made up of the Karst limestone plateau, a physiographic entity that is far more Balkan than Alpine in character.)

Whether or not grounded in geographical reality, widespread acceptance of an attractive national image is an important objective of state policy in Slovenia. That this should be so partly reflects the significance of the tourist industry to Slovenia: in 1993, tourism earned the country the equivalent of USD 800 million in hard currency and was the largest single earner of foreign exchange.[7] Image, no doubt, is also important when it comes to attracting foreign direct investment.

But even if we accept that Slovenia has much in common with Western Europe, the fact remains that the country was until recently a constituent republic of the predominantly Balkan state of Yugoslavia. Today, as in the recent past, the Balkans continue to cast a shadow over Slovenia.

One of the many factors driving the movement for independence in Slovenia (as well as in neighbouring Croatia) was widespread resentment over the transfer of wealth within Yugoslavia from the relatively prosperous north (before independence, Slovenia was easily the wealthiest of the six republics) to the poor and underdeveloped south. In the opinion of the Croatian economist Mate Babić: 'Being inextricably involved with the Serbian economy, which appears to be fuelled by lotus leaves, had a damaging long-term effect on the Croat and Slovene economies.'[8]

But however beneficial severance of connections with Serbia and her allies may be in the long run, in the short term (and especially since the imposition of UN trade sanctions on Serbia and her allies in the summer of 1992) Slovenia has suffered considerably from the loss of a protected market (one that amounted to twenty-two million people) and has been deprived of a guaranteed supply of cheap raw materials from the southern republics of the former Yugoslavian state. Foreign trade is gradually being reoriented northwards, but it will take many years before commerce with the EU states can fully compensate for the lost trade with former Yugoslavia.

And of course trade is by no means the only issue that causes tension between Slovenia and former Yugoslavia. The high degree of ethnic uniformity within Slovenia alone makes it highly unlikely that the country will be drawn directly into the armed conflict raging to the south. Be that as it may, the conflict has from time to time approached dangerously close to Slovenia's borders. Karlovac, scene of bloody fighting between Croats and Serbs in 1991, lies less than fifteen kilometres from the Slovenian frontier. The north-western extremity of the boundary between Croatia and Bosnia-Herzegovonia (the same part of the boundary that partly surrounds the Bihać enclave) lies only fifty kilometres south of the Slovenian–Croatian frontier. These are disturbing geographical realities, the more so considering that the

UN arms embargo applies just as much to Slovenia as it does to the other former constituent republics of Yugoslavia.

In 1992, some 70,000 refugees were admitted into southern Slovenia (after which the border between Slovenia and Croatia was closed to further refugee crossings). Refugees are cared for here and elsewhere in Slovenia, often in former Yugoslav army barracks, at an annual cost equivalent to USD 250 million.[9] At the very least, the continuing conflicts in former Yugoslavia will cause further waves of refugees to press against the Slovenia frontier; in such circumstances, Western European countries might well put strong pressure on Slovenia to admit more people fleeing from the troubled south (for example, Kosovo). Whether the Slovenian economy can cope with heavy influxes of refugees is very much open to question. More importantly, it is difficult to see how Slovenia can indefinitely follow a foreign policy that seemingly turns its back on the Balkans.

Meanwhile, problems confront Slovenia closer to home. Two long-standing disputes of a local kind mar relations between Slovenia and Croatia. One concerns the financing of the jointly run Krško nuclear power station, and the other the demarcation of the maritime frontier between the two states in the Gulf of Piran. These disputes are probably capable of being resolved through continued negotiation.

More complicated and potentially more troublesome is the relationship between Slovenia and Italy. In his chapter here, Sanguin has touched on the complicated twentieth-century history of the border between Slovenia and Italy, and has noted the exodus of the Italian population from Istria in the 1950s. Sanguin is highly informative on the Slovenian safeguards that have been put in place to protect the interests of the Italian minority population living along the south-western border of Slovenia. Unfortunately, the tension between Slovenia and Italy concerns not the Italian-speaking people of Slovenia, but Istrian expatriates and other Italians who believe that they have a legitimate claim to property in Slovenia.

Although Slovenia is willing to uphold the Yugoslavian promise of financial compensation (made in 1983) to these Italian claimants, Italy sees the situation differently. The former Berlusconi government, a coalition government in which the MSI or neo-fascist party formed an important component, argued that the Italian claimants had the same legal rights as Slovenes when it came to the purchase of property taken from them by the former Yugoslavian state. Trieste, where the MSI has made conspicuous advances in local elections, seems to have emerged as a centre for irredentist extremists (still very much in a minority) who make strident claims concerning the restitution of the pre-war frontiers between Italy, Slovenia and Croatia — a boundary demarcation that gave Mussolini's Italy most of the Istrian peninsula.

In October 1994, matters took an unfortunate turn when talks held at Aquilea between Italy and Slovenia produced a compromise agreement (to which a lame-duck Slovenian foreign minister was party) that was later overturned by the Slovenian government. Italy retaliated by threatening to block the Slovenian application for the award of EU associate status, an award that Slovenia had hoped would be made in January 1995. Thus a quarrel over irredentist claims — a species of dispute more familiar in the Balkans than in Western Europe — has come to frustrate the key objective of Slovenian foreign policy, namely closer association with the European Union.

Conclusion

As even a cursory reading of Klemenčić's chapter will indicate, by comparison with most of Eastern Europe Slovenia is unusually well endowed so far as domestic opportunities for economic growth are concerned. In the foregoing, I have attempted to draw attention to one of these opportunities, namely the prevalence of small manufacturing businesses, many of which are located in the countryside. Judging from the experience of Japan, Taiwan and Italy, such enterprises can contribute usefully to economic growth and at the same time can help to reduce disparities in the geographical distribution of wealth.

Though much no doubt still needs to be done as regards privatization and restructuring, domestic economic distortions are probably far less of a constraint on future growth than difficulties in the relationships between Slovenia and neighbouring countries. Slovenia, I have argued, cannot easily turn her back on the Balkans: inconvenient though the reality may be for the government's attempt to promote the image of Slovenia as a Central European republic on the sunny southern slopes of the Alps, the continuing unpredictable situation in former Yugoslavia lies perilously close to Slovenia's southern frontier. In these circumstances, it is especially ironic that Slovenian association with the EU, membership of which is the chief aim of Slovenian foreign policy, should be thwarted not by a Balkan neighbour but by a country — Italy — which is itself an important member of the European Union.

In the interests of achieving faster and more successful economic growth, Slovenia urgently needs better access to the markets of the EU. The dispute with Italy therefore needs to be settled as a matter of priority. In this regard, much depends on whether or not the MSI will influence the government in Italy, and on the extent to which Slovenia will be able successfully to win German and, after January 1995, Austrian support for her cause.

Notes

1 *Financial Times*, 30 March 1992 ('Republic of Slovenia' supplement).
2 K. Natek et al. (1994), *Discover Slovenia*, Ljubljana: Cankarjeva Založba, p. 38.
3 For a discussion of the role of SMEs in contemporary Japan, see H.T. Patrick and T.P. Rohlen (1987), 'Small-scale Family Enterprises', in K. Yamamura and Y. Yasuba (eds), *The Political Economy of Japan. Volume 1: The Domestic Transformation*, Stanford, CA, pp. 331–84; and K.E. Calder (1988), *Crisis and Compensation: Public Policy and Political Stability in Japan 1949–1986*, Princeton, NJ, pp. 312–48.
4 See G. Ranis (1979), 'Industrial Development', in W. Galenson (ed.), *Economic Growth and Structural Change in Taiwan*, Ithaca, NY, pp. 206–62.
5 Reference to the role of small business in Italian manufacturing is made by J. Grimond, 'Awaiting an Alternative: A Survey of Italy', *The Economist*, 26 May 1990.
6 'The Sunny Side of the Alps' is the title of one of the current publications of the government of Slovenia; *The Economist* has referred to Slovenia as 'an *Alpine republic* that borders on Italy, Austria, Hungary and Croatia' (26 June 1993, my italics). See also Edward Mortimer, writing in the *Financial Times* of 9 November 1994: 'Slovenia with its lush Alpine scenery and evident prosperity feels like a southward extension of Austria, only with much lower prices'.
7 *Financial Times*, 12 April 1994 ('Slovenia' supplement).
8 Babić's view is retailed by Misha Glenny (1993), *The Fall of Yugoslavia*, London, revised edn, pp. 63–4.
9 *Financial Times*, 30 March 1993.

13 Which Transition? Some Thoughts on 'Some Features and Problems of the Transformation Process in Slovakia' by Ján Paulov

ADRIAN SMITH

There can be little doubt that it is a fascinating time to be an analyst of change in Central and Eastern Europe. This certainly holds true for one working on contemporary change in Slovakia, and so, given the relative lack of work currently being carried out by Western geographers in Slovakia, Ján Paulov's chapter provides a useful introduction to some of the major issues involved in socio-economic change. The comments I want to make on his chapter are broadly twofold. First, I want to highlight some issues at a more abstract level about how we can understand the nature of socio-spatial change in Slovakia and Central and Eastern Europe; and secondly, I want to provide a more specific consideration of the Slovak context, emphasizing the importance of regional economic fragmentation.

The first point I would like to make is that I completely agree that recognizing the complexity of the transformation is paramount. Back in the heady days of 1989 and 1990 the dominant discourse was such that people like Francis Fukuyama were asserting that the universal trend around the world, and especially in the light of the 'revolutions' in Eastern Europe, was towards stable capitalist liberal democracies. Such positive and uni-linear notions of 'transition' are today, I hope, less pervasive. We are beginning to realize that such profound sets of changes as we are presently witnessing throughout the region are indeed complex. Election results alone are suggesting that the initial euphoria over democratization and economic change are being met, in the face of profound social and economic inequalities and hardships, with more sober assessments of the situation by the electorates of the region. Furthermore, explanations of the divergent experiences of economic transformation (or lack of transformation) have turned towards a context-dependent analysis of 'path dependence' (Stark, 1992; Good, 1994; Bryant and Mokrzycki, 1994b) and 'social embeddedness' (Grabher, 1994; Smith and Swain, 1995; Smith, 1995) in uneven development, rather than an overly simplistic counterposing of command economy replaced by capitalist market economy.

While agreeing that the transformation is complex, however, I think we need to move a step further by saying that transformations are also highly contested by different social groups and characterized by particular strategies adopted by social agents within the context of the economic and social structures of a society. It is only through considering social change as a contested process that we can begin to say anything about what causes the nature of the 'transitions' in Slovakia and more broadly in Central and Eastern Europe. If we are indeed witnessing a transition to capitalism, which I believe is a highly uneven process and a problematic claim, then we need to identify the particular paths such a transition is taking. If we only resort to identifying particular policy measures which may or may not have the desired effect of establishing capitalist social relations, we could miss some of the vital processes that are actually structuring socio-spatial change in the region. In this sense, I believe the first question we need to ask ourselves is 'which transition' or even 'which transformation?' (Bryant and Mokrzycki, 1994a).

In addressing such questions it is useful to start with what is driving the changes occurring in contemporary Slovakia. By this I mean what social forces and social relations are structuring change, and how these social relations represent the strategies of different social groups (labour, the central state, the local state, emerging forms of capital and so on). As geographers, it is also useful to ask what these changing social relations mean for the nature of socio-spatial change. Professor Paulov begins to hint at some of these towards the end of his summary by introducing the questions of, for example, the 'geographical position of Slovakia' and, I think most importantly, the 'regional differentiation of the transformation process'.

The second point I wish to make regards what I would consider as the over-concentration on policy measures. Professor Paulov is correct to identify the sets of policy reforms (changes to property rights, price reforms, foreign trade reform and so on) that do indeed resemble the form taken by such policies in Western capitalist democracies. But it is perhaps more enlightening to look at the emergence of divergent strategies for development which underlie particular policy positions, rather than looking at the 'transition' as one in which all we need to do is to introduce a set of policy measures to create a uni-linear path to capitalism. What I am arguing for is an approach which identifies divergent strategies, and attempts to examine these in the context of power relations; that is, which strategies are dominant and why?

Let me provide an example from the Slovak context to make this clearer which draws upon my own research on industrial change and regional economic development in Slovakia. What I want to consider is the question of regional economic fragmentation in the Slovak space-economy, or what Professor Paulov calls 'regional differentiation of the transformation process'. I consider this problem to be the most pressing long-term structural problem facing Slovakia. It will have profound implications for the nature of any transition to capitalism, particularly because it is creating sets of economic and regional 'winners' and 'losers', although I realize that such dualistic divisions are an over-simplification of a complex reality comprising divergent transformatory pathways. In addition, profound regional fragmentation is occurring within the context of forty years of some kind of regional economic convergence in which material conditions (albeit of a particular and somewhat distorted kind) improved for the vast majority (Smith, 1996).

We can identify three main forms of regional economic differentiation, or what I would prefer to call uneven development (Smith, 1994, 1995, 1996). First, there are three, or possibly four (if we include Košice, which I am uncertain about) metropolitan cores, exhibiting the ability to transform themselves into centres of economic dynamism (Bratislava and its hinterland, Banská Bystrica and Žilina). Secondly, there are the 'crisis regions' — the branch plant economies of the northern, southern and eastern border regions established in the latter days of state socialism, and the agricultural peripheries in the south and the east. Here we find unemployment already reaching 25 per cent — higher for more peripheralized groups such as Romanies and in particular pockets of economic collapse. Thirdly, we find a set of more intermediate regions somewhere between these extremes where the future is uncertain and where the processes of contested change that I alluded to earlier are most apparent. But if these are the major geo-economic patterns, what strategies underlie the relative success of some areas and the collapse of others? What can this tell us about the processes structuring the creation of capitalism?

If we look first at the metropolitan cores, especially the Bratislava region, one of the striking developments that make these areas the most dynamic is the development of a model of growth based upon finance and trading. Bratislava, for example, has the highest concentration of new firm formation, and many of these firms are involved in banking, business services and trade (Brhel, 1994). As such, they represent a regional strategy based on the circulation of rents derived from the industrial sector, rather than industrial growth — a kind of speculative development strategy (see Dunford and Fielding, 1997, for a discussion of a similar growth strategy in the south-east of England). Whether this represents a transformation to capitalism is an open question. It certainly contains elements of it — for example, market speculation strategies. Professor Paulov raises the issue of regional policy in relation to the Bratislava–Vienna region. Given that Bratislava already registers four times the national average gross domestic product (Smith, 1996), the current emphasis on the creation of inter-regional linkages in the 'Golden Triangle' of Vienna–Bratislava–Györ (Mojzes and Slimak, 1993; Schneidewind, 1993; Tompai, 1993) seems somewhat curious. Regional policies, surely, should be directed towards those areas and social groups most in need. While there are no doubt many such groups within the Slovak part of the 'Golden Triangle' (evidenced by increasing levels of homelessness and social marginality as house and property prices increase and job markets are restructured), there are many more in the most peripheral and increasingly deindustrialized regions which I will now turn to.

Contrasted to this relative dynamism is the selective collapse of the more peripheral, branch plant regional economies. The major dynamic at work here is not the growth of a local capitalism but the shedding of branch plants by core enterprises as the structure of industrial integration collapses, and the painful adaptation to market conditions (remembering that markets do not necessarily equal capitalism). As well as creating some of the highest levels of regional unemployment, these regions are also those with some of the lowest levels of new firm formation (Hospodárska rada vlády SR, 1993). Therefore, these regions represent the result of strategies for deindustrialization through the disintegration of the regulative system of state socialist enterprise integration (the industrial association system).

Finally, there are a large number of more intermediate regions whose fortunes are yet to be decided. Here some of the most apparent forms of contested social relations can be found. To take one example — that of Central Slovak regions dependent on the formerly dominant armaments sector — we find divergent strategies between (a) mercantilist forces seeking to gain advantage in the local economy through buying and selling the inputs and products of large, increasingly debt-ridden heavy engineering enterprises; (b) the survival strategies of these state enterprises; and (c) new productive capital faced with large tax bills partly resulting from continued state subsidization of these large enterprises and little support from banks because of the latter's speculative strategies (see Smith, 1994, 1995, 1996 for more detail on these divergent strategies). Socio-economic change is indeed complex!

Therefore, while there are a number of *policy* problems that Slovakia faces, I would argue that it is more profitable, in terms of our understanding of socio-spatial change, to consider the dynamics *underlying* the present patterns of uneven development that are now so apparent in the space-economy. This demands an approach which not only identifies certain empirical and spatial regularities, but also attempts to unearth the relationships between structure and strategy in regional economic change.

References

Brhel, J. (1994), *Malé a stredné podnikanie*, Bratislava.

Bryant, C. and Mokrzycki, E. (eds) (1994a), *The New Great Transformation?*, London.

Bryant, C. and Mokrzycki, E. (1994b), 'Introduction: Theorizing the Changes in East-Central Europe', in C. Bryant, and E. Mokrzycki (eds.), *The New Great Transformation?*, London, pp. 1–11.

Dunford, M. and Fielding, A. (1997), 'Greater London, the South East region and the Wider Britain: Metropolitan Polarisation, Uneven Development and Interregional Migration', in H. Blötevogel, and A. Fielding (eds.), *People, Jobs and Mobility in the New Europe*, Chichester.

Good, D. (1994), 'The Economic Transformation of Central and Eastern Europe in Historical Perspective: Main Themes and Issues', in D. Good (ed.), *Economic Transformation in East and Central Europe: Legacies from the Past and Policies for the Future*, London, pp. 3–24.

Grabher, G. (1994), 'The Elegance of Incoherence: Institutional Legacies, Privatization and Regional Development in East Germany and Hungary', *WZB Discussion Papers*, FS 1, pp. 94–103.

Hospodárska rada vlády SR (1993), *Regionálna politika vlády SR a návrh vládnych programov štrukturálnej adaptacie regiónov*, Bratislava.

Mojzes, M. and Slimak, D. (1993), 'Project on Transboundary Co-operation between Market Economies and Economies in Transition: The Role of the ECE Project Vienna–Bratislava–Győr', in *The Challenges Facing European Society with the Approach of the Year 2000: Transborder Co-operation Within Sustainable Regional/Spatial Planning in Central Europe*, Council of Europe, European Regional Planning, 55, Strasbourg.

Schneidewind, P. (1993), 'Regional Planning for the City-Triangle Vienna–Bratislava–Győr: Experiences and Expectations', in *The Challenges Facing European Society with the Approach of the Year 2000: Transborder Co-operation Within Sustainable Regional/Spatial Planning in Central Europe*, Council of Europe, European Regional Planning, 55, Strasbourg.

Smith, A. (1994), 'Uneven Development and the Restructuring of the Armaments Industry in Slovakia', *Transactions*, Institute of British Geographers, vol. 19, no. 4, pp. 404–24.

Smith, A (1995), 'Regulation Theory, Strategies of Enterprise Integration and the Political Economy of Regional Economic Restructuring in Central and Eastern Europe: The Case of Slovakia', *Regional Studies*, vol. 29, no. 8, pp. 765–76.

Smith, A. (1996), 'From Convergence to Fragmentation: Uneven Development, Industrial Restructuring and the "Transition to Capitalism" in Slovakia', *Environment and Planning A*, vol. 28, no. 1, pp. 135–56.

Tompai, G (1993), 'The Vienna–Bratislava–Győr Conurbation', in *The Challenges Facing European Society with the Approach of the Year 2000: Transborder Co-operation*

Within Sustainable Regional/Spatial Planning in Central Europe, Council of Europe, European Regional Planning, 55, Strasbourg.

Žarská, E. (1993), 'Vyvoj mobility obyvatel'stva v priestore Bratislava–Viedeň', *Hospodárske noviny*, 11 June, p. 4.

14 Privatization in Romania, with Particular Reference to the Rural Areas

DAVID TURNOCK

Introduction

Romania has shown little interest in shock therapy and the pace of market reform has been leisurely, which is hardly surprising in view of the very high level of centralization under the Communist system (Ben-Ner and Montias, 1991). Ambivalence might be linked with the political complexion of Romanian governments which have have been in power since the revolution (Tismaneanu, n.d.). Former Communist Party members are prominent in the new regime and elements in the governing Party of Social Democracy (PSD), formerly the Democratic National Salvation Front, may wish to combine a slow relaxation of state ownership with increased personal involvement in the economic sphere. Yet there was no opposition at all before 1989: only a handful of dissidents isolated from the population and from each other (Roper, 1994). Now the democratic process is operating and the president's party has succeeded in gaining the trust of the electorate. Meanwhile the opposition Democratic Convention (DC) 'has yet to convince many Romanians it is a viable alternative to the ruling party or to capitalise fully on the government's unpopularity' (Marsh and Done, 1995, p. 33).

The new civil society is generally apprehensive about a market economy (Hoffman, 1991; Kligman, 1990). In view of the sacrifices demanded by Communism, people will not accept 'that it would be good to sacrifice themselves [again] for the sake of future generations' (Nicolaescu, 1993, p. 602). So while the principle of free competition may be acceptable as an ideal, most people hesitate to 'replace government control with more seriously binding controls that are inflicted by market-related institutions' (ibid., pp. 103–4). For radical reorganization of all the state-owned enterprises would almost certainly generate unacceptable levels of unemployment, in the context of a limited social security system (Hoffman, 1992). Meanwhile, in agriculture there is a presumption (fed to no small extent by government propaganda) that unfettered market forces would drive many smallholders out of business and result in much larger capitalist holdings, perhaps controlled by the landowners who were expropriated after the First World War and whose claims might be accepted under the more generous restitution terms promised by the opposition. The dilemma, however, is that while Romanians do not want radical change, they remain dissatisfied with wages that average just 100 US dollars per month (only two-thirds of the 1989 level).

Of course there are variations in political outlook. While the PSD is strong in Moldavia and Wallachia the opposition DC (a group of parties associated with the National Peasant Party) polls well in Banat, Bucharest and parts of Transylvania. The DC also maintains contact with the Hungarian Democratic Union, which attracts the overwhelming support of the Hungarian minority in Transylvania. There are also substantial Romanian nationalist parties, however ('Romania Mare' in Moldavia and Wallachia and the Romanian National Unity Party in Transylvania), which are broadly sympathetic towards to the PSD. This leaves the National Salvation Front (NSF), which broke away from President Iliescu just before the 1992 election. Despite a record of relatively rapid reform going back to the early days of the revolution, when Petre Roman was prime minister, it has not so far been able to make common cause with the mainstream opposition. Some observers therefore see a schism between a minority conception of Euro-Atlantic integration and a majority view which inclines towards a nationalistic oligarchic regime that is relatively isolated internationally. People of the latter persuasion still want to see interventionist policies from their government, backed by a strong presidential leader (Turnock and Turnock, 1995).

Market Reforms in Industry

The Romanian government has taken a cautious approach towards the reorganization and privatization of industry. Elements within the government may have vested interests but, at the same time, the largest section of public opinion favours very gradual change in restructuring industry and in removing subsidies (still very substantial for public transport and the postal service). Productivity levels remain low in many enterprises where workers may take paid leave on a rota basis in order to avoid higher unemployment. Many enterprises were hardly viable even before the revolution when the economy comprised 'an incoherent structure of different sectors with an autarchic reactionary pattern; generating inefficient activites and constantly declining living standards' (Nicolaescu, 1993, p. 102). Industry continues to be a heavy drain on the country's finances, especially heavy industry with its high manning levels and heavy energy consumption. Restructuring is therefore a major challenge (Florea, 1992) and it is a moot point whether a rather more vigorous reorganization would not open the way for retraining and thereby ensure a supply of labour for an expanding private sector, which is what the opposition claim.

The private sector is certainly expanding and now controls 37 per cent of the economy. To attract investment the country has a substantial raw material base, a large domestic market (albeit with limited spending power at the present time) and is well situated for trade with Central Europe, the Middle East, North Africa and the former Soviet Union successor states. The Danube highway is an important part of the infrastructure and could be harnessed as a commercial corridor between Western Europe and both the former Soviet Union and the Middle East. But foreign capital is urgently needed since the payment of a 30 billion US dollar foreign debt during the 1980s reduced financial resources and created blockages. Investors were deterred, however, by the shrinkage of the economy by 40 per cent between 1990 and 1992, due to reduced domestic demand and the collapse of Comecon. Industry (which remains 90 per cent state-owned) continued to produce for stock, with generally low profits. Investors were also deterred by a bureaucratic business environment, corruption and political uncertainty, as the government (with supporters prominent in the economy, the judiciary and the media) has depended on the more extremist xenophobic parties. The latter have opposed a bilaterial treaty with Hungary that would safeguard minority rights and thereby satisfy one of the preconditions for eventual EU and NATO membership.

Romania did, however, achieve considerable macroeconomic stability by 1995. Inflation came down from 300 per cent in 1993 to 62 per cent in 1994 and reached 25–30 per cent in 1995. Moreover, as the economy moved into a growth of 3.4 per cent in 1994, with a greatly improved export performance, depeciation of the leu (by 36 per cent in 1994) fell well below the inflation rate. The state budget has grown to 15 billion lei and progess is now being rewarded with a greater inflow of money from abroad. There are loans from international financial insti-tutions (to which most of the 4.8 billion US dollars of foreign debt is owed), and money that went initially for consumption is being used increasingly for investment and hard currency reserves. Romania has also returned to international capital markets, securing a 150 million US dollar loan from Citibank in 1995. Foreign investment has meanwhile increased from USD 87.3 million in 1990 to USD 650.5 million in 1994 (a total of USD 1.27 billion over the five years). The number of countries involved had risen from 68 to 116 (as Romania has extended its business contacts into South America and South-East Asia) and the number of companies from 1,427 to 10,703. Most prominent is the Daewoo (South Korea) investment of USD 900 million to upgrade the 'Oltcit' (Craiova) car factory in which it has a 51 per cent stake. But the company also had plans for shipbuilding, tourism and infrastructure.

Much of the foreign investment (regulated by decree in 1990 and legislation in 1991) has gone into joint ventures linking foreign and domestic enterprises. Some 70 per cent falls to relatively large projects involving sums of more than one million dollars. Prior to the Daewoo investment a major geographical imbalance emerged with almost two-thirds of the capital in such projects destined for Bucharest, while another quarter was directed to seven provincial towns (Bistriţa, Hateg, Iaşi, Oradea, Otelu Roşu, Râmnicu Valcea and Zălău). The remaining 10 per cent was distributed among nineteen other locations, three of which were villages (Guran, 1994), and more of Romania's 250 towns will probably benefit in due course. The possible introduction of customs-free zones has also been discussed (Caraiani, 1991; Miron, 1991). Rural areas are also likely to attract a proportion of the foreign investment, especially in relation to the smaller projects. Studies of foreign investment in the Romanian countryside have revealed a large number of projects (many of them initiated by émigré Romanians wishing to support their former home areas) but spatial imbalance is also a striking feature. Talanga (1995) has shown that while 10.7 million dollars were invested in rural areas up to the beginning of 1993 (1.04 dollars per capita), 5.9 million dollars went to the Bucharest area (5.6 dollars per capita — 15.4 in Ilfov) and another 2.6 million went to Banat–Crisana–Maramureş (1.8 dollars per capita). This suggests that Romania will need to rely on capital and enterprise generated within the country. And this attaches great importance to programmes for the encouragement of small business incubation. The Ministry of Research and Technology is co-ordinating the project which is creating space (by arrangement with universities and other institutions) in an increasing number of county towns as well as the capital city (Fiedler, 1992).

Meanwhile, privatization of Romanian industry is accepted in principle. But making enterprises attractive for private investment will involve radical surgery which the government is only slowly beginning to contemplate (Briggs, 1993). The limited supply of money available through the banking system has been seen as a formidable barrier (Nicolaescu, 1993 pp. 105–6). Some progress has of course been made through employee–management buy-outs, but such deals can be arranged primarily as political transactions, handing over government ownership of assets and, at the same time, ending the government's responsibility towards the workforce. But the government has declared it will not 'sell' the country's assets to foreign interests wholesale; while there is little indication that Romanians as a whole are either keen to own shares or have the money to buy them. The offer of 'ownership certificates' by the Stolojan government, under the privatization law of 1991 (at a symbolic price of 100 lei), led to many subsequent sales to speculators who have now found the value of the certificates diminishing through inflation. For although the privatization process got under way in 1992, with the offering of shares in a state-owned brewery, only 137 of the 791 companies listed for privatization in 1993 have actually passed into the private sector.

A more ambitious scheme was announced by the Vacaroiu government in 1994, to be based on a further offering of vouchers (actually called coupons) and covering 2,928 companies: the residue of 654 from the first round along with 2,274 others. Indeed, in its final form this mass privatization is affecting 3,300 companies, operating in all sectors and in all parts of the country. Although some of these companies have not been making any profit (according to advertisements which appeared in the Romanian press in 1994) privatization was expected within two years, compared with the seven envisaged for the first round. The programme has certainly been strongly encouraged by the World Bank, as a precondition for further loan payments, because it should enhance the macro-economic climate and stimulate company managements to become more entrepreneurial. After careful preparation the programme got underway in August 1995. People were to receive privatization coupons for a nominal sum and then had to select the company in which a shareholding was desired, a process to be handled through a network of computers in post offices. To prevent speculation the coupons were to be negotiable only by the people to whom they were allocated in the first place. Certificates were issued by the end of March 1996. Meanwhile, foreigners can buy shares for cash through application to the State Ownership Fund (with the help, if necessary, of the Romanian Agency for Development and/or the Romanian Agency for Privatization).

Privatization in Agriculture

In one respect, the Romanian economy has experienced profound change because there has been a major transfer of ownership in agriculture. State farms have remained largely intact, but most farm land previously belonging to the co-operative farms has been privatized. Immediately after the revolution it was decreed that each family in the rural areas would receive 1.0 hectares of land (0.5 hectares in the case of state farm workers). Then former owners were invited to submit claims for restitution up to a maximum of 10.0 hectares arable equivalent. These measures were extremely popular, given the widespread disenchantment with the co-operatives (in contrast to countries like Hungary and Slovakia where results were usually considered satisfactory). Peasants were euphoric over the return of their land and in the hill and mountain regions unilateral action was geared to regaining exactly the same plots that families had previously been forced to surrender. In many villages therefore the pre-Communist cadaster was restored, complete with its patterns of fragmentation.

Agriculture is being restructured (Davidovici, 1991; Zoican, 1992). The immediate response to privatization appeared to be negative, with a further outflow of population and a collapse in production that was evident in both the crop and livestock sectors (Parpala, 1992b). Much of the migration noted during 1990, however, reflected merely the official recognition of transfers which had taken place earlier when controls were in force: the situation now is much more stable. And the crisis in production is being gradually overcome, with 1995 a particularly good year. A new market system is emerging (with the help of EU 'Phare' funding) and should limit the retreat into subsistence farming. In the particular case of livestock rearing (Iosif, 1991 and 1994c), the problems of low-quality animals inherited from the co-operatives are being overcome and a rational correlation is being made with the available fodder supply (Turnock, 1993). It is, however, difficult for farmers to compete with imports and there are suggestions that the involvement of politicians in trading companies is resulting in unnecessary importing, particularly by the 'Romcereal' monopoly which is buying imported cereal while declining what some Romanian farmers are able to offer.

The Romanian village is witnessing restrained growth as farmers spend their modest incomes and some migrants return from the towns and establish small businesses, overwhelmingly in the tertiary sector (Ianoş, 1995). Farmers are making rational decisions with regard to the market: considering the available labour, the physical potential of their land and the local marketing situation (Mironiuc, 1994). Where non-agricultural employment is limited it is logical for farmers to invest their labour by working smallholdings as intensively as possible. Some informal co-operation is usual: for example a rota system for the herding of livestock on the common grazings. And in arable farming areas co-ordination in the use of machinery and in the application of fertilisers has led to the growth of associations, strongly supported by the state (Fratila, 1992; Parpala, 1993). Associations provide an ideal solution for households (especially those living in urban areas) that lack the labour to work a holding properly. There is also an opportunity for households with a labour surplus seeking an outlet, although informal sharecropping arrangements can also be negotiated. At present there is great deal of experimentation as individual farmers assess the merits of association (as opposed to independent operations) and also note the performance of different associations within their communities (Bordanc, 1995; Ianoş et al., 1992).

The Farming Future in the Romanian Carpathians

The distinctive nature of the Carpathian area has been widely discussed. In the rural areas agriculture is fundamental. The emphasis is traditionally on livestock rearing in the context of pluriactivity, with farming households combining work on the land with activity in forestry, mining and industry (Turnock, 1992). Young people still make every effort to find a job outside agriculture, even when this involves long periods of absence from the farm (traditionally the case in Maramureş). Wives run the farms and much of the crop-land may be used for hay. People of middle age will tend to be more active in agriculture, fully exploiting the potential of the smallholding by cropping both their outlying strips and the land around the secondary farmsteads characteristic of the Subcarpathian areas of Buzău and Vrancea, despite the social costs arising through absence from the main family home during the growing season. Farm work may be complemented by casual work or farm diversification. Meanwhile, older people will struggle to manage their farm, often depending on informal local arrangements and occasional visits by younger family members.

With the restitution of agricultural land and the demise of the co-operatives important questions arise for the future of the Carpathian countryside (Ianoş, 1995). An optimist looking for a rapid transition to West European conditions might envisage the 'best scenario' in terms of the privatization of non-agricultural enterprises and a considerable growth of new business underpinned by émigré capital and return migration of Romanian workers from the towns. In other words, private enterprise would blossom and decades of under-investment in the rural areas would be corrected. On the other hand, the 'worst scenario' would see the relative backwardness of rural conditions reinforced by capital shortage, limited privatization and a decline in commercial activity, as well as a disgruntled peasantry disappointed by the land restitution programme and the assistance provided by the local authorities. Field study in seven small districts, inspired by the tradition of Romanian social survey (Golopentia and Georgescu, 1942), was expected to reveal a range of regional situations exemplifying, in varying degrees, the potentials and problems associated with economic change.

Table 14.1 Migration in seven Carpathian districts, 1986–93

District	1986				1990				1991–93 Annual Averages				
a	A	B	C	E	A	B	C	E	A	B	C	D	E
Aries	606	1241	-635	-11.1	537	2164	-1627	-30.1	345	1091	-746	28.5	-13.8
Urban	319	221	+98	+6.4	319	406	-87	-5.8	220	246	-26	28.5	-1.77
Rural	287	1020	-733	-17.5	218	1758	-1540	-40.1	125	845	-720	28.5	-18.7
Lapuş	1098	2323	-1225	-7.1	927	4742	-3815	-23.1	708	2625	-1917	20.2	-11.8
Urban	566	869	-303	-4.7	456	1935	-1479	-24.4	333	877	-543	19.9	-8.0
Rural	532	1454	-922	-8.5	471	2807	-2336	-22.4	375	1748	-1373	20.3	-13.1
Lotru	679	1138	-459	-6.1	911	3481	-2570	-31.1	766	1245	-479	24.3	-5.8
Urban	347	272	+75	+2.8	504	674	-170	-5.9	396	314	+82	24.7	+2.9
Rural	332	866	-534	-9.2	407	2807	-2400	-44.5	370	931	-561	24.1	-10.4
Nehoiu	345	1076	-731	-7.9	1113	4782	-3669	-40.3	875	1661	-786	27.8	-8.6
Urban	35	90	-55	-4.6	504	674	-170	-5.9	181	131	+50	24.6	+3.9
Rural	310	986	-676	-8.4	609	4108	-3499	-44.6	694	1530	-836	28.3	-10.7
Reşiţa	2608	3751	-1143	-6.1	3006	6461	-3455	-20.4	2519	3099	-580	33.2	-3.4
Urban	2533	3432	-899	-5.7	2202	5234	-3032	-21.3	2209	2551	-342	33.4	-2.4
Rural	75	319	-244	-8.1	804	1227	-423	-15.8	310	548	-238	32.0	-8.9
Retezat	3993	3249	+744	+3.6	7776	7254	+522	+2.4	4900	4013	+887	41.5	+4.1
Urban	3765	2981	+784	+4.7	7468	6471	+997	+5.6	4596	3496	+1100	45.2	+6.1
Rural	228	268	-40	-1.0	308	783	-475	-13.2	304	517	-213	22.8	-5.9
Topliţa	469	612	-143	-2.8	452	1168	-716	-14.0	327	552	-225	16.9	-4.4
Urban	216	221	-5	-0.2	248	515	-267	-13.2	154	217	-63	17.6	-3.1
Rural	253	391	-138	-4.5	204	653	-449	-14.5	173	335	-162	16.4	-5.2

A = persons moving in; B = persons moving out; C = migration balance; D = turnover per thousand of the total population; E = net migration per thousand.

Note

a Location of districts are indicated by the relevant county — and town where it is different from the name chosen for the district: Aries (Campeni, Alba County); Lapuş (Targu Lapuş, Maramureş County); Lotru (Brezoi, Valcea County); Nehoiu (Buzău County); Reşiţa (Caraş-Severin County); Retezat (Hateg/Petrosani, Hunedoara County); Topliţa (Harghita County).

Source: Commune files.

Net out-migration from the rural areas seems to be slowing down after the high levels experienced in 1990 (when it is possible that many earlier moves were first registered) (see Table 14.1). The overall picture was -13.23 in 1991, -11.99 in 1992 and -8.04 in 1993 (close to the figure of -8.43 in 1986). The level of movement (in and out combined) remains high. In the towns the high level of 58.3 per thousand for 1990 has fallen to an average of 34.6 for 1991–3 (close to the 1986 figure of 34.3), while in the rural areas the high level of 46.5 in 1990 has fallen to an average of 24.2 in 1991–

2, rather than the 18.8 recorded in 1986. Out-migration is compounded by natural decrease in many areas. In the seven Carpathian areas only Lapuş was still showing natural increase in 1991–93: Aries, Lotru, Nehoiu and Topliţa showed natural increase in 1986 and 1990 but changed to natural decrease in 1991–93. There seems to be a demographic transition working through the mountain region, moving towards smaller families and higher proportions of non-active people. Family size remains relatively high in the north (for example, Lapuş) and in small areas of the west (like Aries) and south-west; while the active population is high in these same areas as well as some easterly areas (like Nehoiu) and south-central areas such as Lotru. This pattern also correlates with levels of agricultural labour.

In Table 14.2 demographic criteria have been combined with other indicators on the economy and infrastructure, in an attempt at synthesis through the identification of clusters of low (↓), average (•) and high (↑) values. Sharply contrasting situations emerge. Retezat and Topliţa have strong economies, relatively strong demographic profiles and good infrastructure. Aries and Nehoiu have weak economies with demographic distortions and poor infrastructure. Lotru emerges in an intermediate position. There are inconsistencies in the cases of Lapuş and Reşiţa. The former shows strength in demography, yet an indifferent economy (it has industrial salaries yet limited production) and very poor infrastructure (apart from the nucleated settlement); Resita has a very good infrastructure but a weak economy and a poor demographic profile. The anomalies arise through the seasonal migrations of people from Lapuş (especially the younger men) and the recent collapse of the Reşiţa heavy industrial base after two centuries of growth. These are matters that should be addressed by rural development strategies, but there is little money available and no clear consensus over priorities. Furthermore, the indications are that rural issues are not a paramount concern now that the peasantry has been effectively neutralized as a political force by land restitution (Kideckel, 1992). The large urban-based state-owned enterprises are likely to have the first call on the government's purse.

There is certainly a need for investment to modernize mountain farms with better buildings and machines which could make major savings in labour and achieve greater efficiency in the livestock sector in terms of both meat and dairy produce. A big improvement in distribution is needed, including better links with the food processors and an improved technical base for an ecologically sustainable agriculture; as discussed in the economic press. But there is nothing to suggest that the peasant farmers will be generously assisted, despite the Vacaroiu government's desire to extend agricultural credit. And, more generally, it is argued that on economic grounds government intervention in agriculture should be resisted, despite the temptations arising from the recent history of central planning and the elaborate arrangements for agriculture in the EU (Karp and Stefanou, 1994).

Table 14.2 Summary profiles of seven Carpathian districts

	Aries	Lapuş	Lotru	Nehoiu	Reşiţa	Retezat	Topliţa
Population							
Natural Increase	•	↑	•	•	↓	↓	•
Female Population*	↓	•	↑	↓	↓	↑	↑
Female Farm Labour*	↓	•	•	↑	↓	↓	•
Average Family Size	↑	↑	↓	↓	•	•	↓
Students	•	↑	•	•	↑	↓	↑
Nursery Places	↓	•	↓	↓	↑	↓	•
Migration: Permanent*	↓	•	•	•	•	↑	↑
Migration: Temporary*	↓	•	•	↓	↑	↑	↑
Pensioners*	↑	↑	↑	•	↓	↓	•
Economy							
Non-Agricultural Employment	↓	↓	•	•	•	•	↑
Unemployment*	↑	•	•	↓	↓	•	↓
Industrial Output Value	•	↓	↓	•	↓	↑	↑
Industry: Salaried Workers	•	↑	•	•	↓	•	↑
Population–Land Ratio	↓	↓	•	•	↑	↑	•
Cereal Area	•	•	•	↓	•	↑	↓
Fruit Production	↑	↓	•	↑	↓	↓	↓
Livestock Density	↑	•	↑	•	↓	•	•
Livestock Reduction*	↓	•	↑	•	↓	↓	•
Infrastructure							
Population Density	•	↑	↓	•	↓	↓	•
Ditto: Built-Up Area	↓	↓	↓	•	↑	•	•
Settlement Nucleation	↓	↑	•	↓	↑	↓	↑
Living Space Per Capita	↓	↓	•	↑	↑	↑	↑
Active Population	↑	•	•	↓	↓	•	•
Population with Salaries	•	↓	•	•	•	↑	↑
State-Owned Housing Stock	↓	↓	↓	↓	↑	↑	•
Television Licences	↓	↓	↑	↑	↑	↑	↑
Commercial/Service Units	•	↓	↑	•	•	↑	•

* For criteria thus marked higher values are rated as less desirable.

For agriculture's problems are not unique and financial assistance should be arranged through banks, with governments remaining at arm's length. So rural sector recovery can only be led by urban demand, with food prices and farm incomes increasing to the point where investment in agriculture once again becomes possible. This would then increase farm incomes and support rural businesses. Regional variations might emerge more strongly, with greater market orientation in Transylvania, perhaps with variations in strategies between the ethnic groups.

Discussion must be linked with wider European issues, for rural areas of Romania cannot be divorced from trends occurring elsewhere (Turnock, 1995). Food production has been complicated not only by domestic upheavals but by the collapse of the former Soviet Union and competition from imported food linked with tariff reforms that anticipate eventual EU membership. Romania and other East European countries may have to abandon expectations of producing more and more food. Although support through the 'Phare' programme is still linked with the classic production philosophy of the Common Agricultural Policy (CAP), thinking within the European Union is veering towards a change of policy which will mean lower levels of support for agriculture in future. This could be beneficial to Eastern Europe in reducing the flow of food (at subsidized prices) into the region at the expense of domestic producers. Over the longer term it would reduce the cost of EU membership and improve Eastern Europe's chances of competing in food production through lower labour costs. Yet the EU dimension emphasizes the importance of continuing structural change to increase efficiency (Repassy and Symes, 1992).

Modernization of small farms through new buildings, mechanization and livestock breeding will be extremely costly (Iosif, 1994a; Surd, 1994), but small units of ownership could combine into larger functional units for farm management (Parpala, 1992a). The question is, will this be done by the farmers themselves through the associations and through kinship groups with joint investment programmes (Iosif, 1994b), or will it be achieved by a new entrepreneurial class, emerging perhaps from the ranks of the state farm managers who may gradually enter the villages to lease (and eventually buy) land which the peasant owners cannot work on their own? Such 'nomenklatura' farms could start to expand once the distribution of definitive titles is complete and there is access to loans at preferential rates. Much of the present farming population would therefore transfer to the secondary and tertiary sectors, as the younger members of peasant households are seeking to do at present. School-leavers show a strong preference for work in industry and the tertiary sector (especially government service).

On this basis the future holds a further decline in the rural population and an acceleration of rural–urban migration. This might be very evident in Lapuş if high levels of out-migration undermine the present healthy age structure in the way that has recently been experienced in Aries. This would certainly be feasible given the size of most provincial towns in Romania today — especially county towns like Campulung and Lugoj which lost their status as a result of reorganization of local government under Communism. This would provide more 'gateway cities' to support regional development in Romania (Ianoş and Talanga, 1994). There are still some historic 'lands' lacking an urban centre and the latest generation of county plans reflect these potentials (Surd, 1991), for example, additional local centres (currently villages) proposed for Bihor county at Popesti, Sambata, Tinca and Vadu Crisului to strengthen the base of urban hierarchy. Of course, these new towns would be backed by the traditional rural settlement system rather than the greatly attenuated structure envisaged under Communist planning.

An alternative approach would be diversification in the rural areas. In the Carpathians, the small farm base is socially fundamental, so diversification may offer a way forward in Romania and in other mountain regions of post-Communist Central Europe. In additional to traditional crafts (Iosif, 1992), the economic press has made much of the potential for farm-based community tourism, based on the charm of Romanian villages (Cianga, 1991). Various localities have been described, with particular attention to the eastern Carpathians and several constituent areas (Talaba, 1991). The ecological factor may also exert an influence on future policy, for mountain areas are experiencing some undesirable landscape changes (Muica and Muica, 1995). Planners have advocated sustainable development and have outlined the implications in terms of a 'green' agriculture, so a future conservation programme to reduce erosion could be tilted in favour of forestry and tourism, with cropping and stocking at today's lower levels of intensity.

Meanwhile, quality products from organic farming could be handled by an enlarged processing sector that could itself create more jobs in rural areas. The indigenous development of local industries and handicrafts has been significant where there are few capital demands, for example the refurbishment of small water-powered mills which can be undertaken by local craftsmen. And in these respects there is a degree of continuity arising from the flexibility shown by some local authorities prior to the revolution. Diversification has also been suggested through small woodcutting enterprises, appropriate in the context of both the large state-owned forests and the small woodland units returned to former owners under a modest programme of restitution (with one hectare as the maximum). There might also be more foreign investment in rural industry, perhaps through light engineering linked with the semi-derelict machine-tractor stations. A good example can be seen in Estelnic in Harghita, where a German clothing company is now providing shift work for women in the district.

Yet a rural social policy is needed, even if there is no blanket subsidy system for agriculture. Infrastructural norms could be laid down and some help could be given to improve housing standards in areas like Lapuş and to extend electricity supplies and roads suitable for motor vehicles to the small villages of Aries. There could be an improved agricultural advisory service and measures to encourage small businesses in rural areas, although many peasants are suspicious of too much state intervention. It is interesting to see that the Agriculture Ministry has set up a Commission for Mountainous Regions with a policy remit to disseminate the principles of 'mountainology' through education and publicity (Turnock, 1994). This follows the thinking of R. Rey, outlined during the Communist era as an alternative to the more uncompromising consolidation envisaged under the prevailing 'sistematizare' policy (Rey, 1979). Its efforts have been complemented by the planning profession in Bucharest, which is looking at physical planning for rural areas with reference to tourism, agricultural development (for example, irrigation), control of erosion (gullying) and expansion of the market system.

Summary and Conclusion

Romania has avoided the radical options which have been adopted in other countries of Eastern Europe. But the reasons for this cautious approach should be sought in the mood of the electorate and not simply in the conservative leanings of the ruling party. After the years of austerity under Communism, Romanians are not prepared to take risks. That opportunities are lost by this strategy cannot be denied, yet the gradualism evident on both the industrial and agricultural fronts provides an element of social security and offers a breathing space, allowing the debate to continue against a background of further information and experience. Romanian industry is now being privatized, although the eventual distribution of holdings between small shareholders as opposed to domestic institutions and foreign interests has yet to be decided.

Meanwhile, in the case of agriculture, privatization has resulted in the creation of thousands of small family farms. This is socially and politically necessary, given the lack of alternative employment and the very limited social security provision. The small farm system provides an equitable response to the land reform challenge and offers security to a population seeking temporary relief from the pressures of state control. The traditional mixed farm is certainly capable of offering modest rewards which will allow for repairs and extensions to houses and limited technical improvements. Farm diversification through a growth of rural industry and agrotourism will be helpful on social grounds in boosting farm incomes, but the national interest will be better served by an efficient agriculture depending on well-trained and highly motivated young people. Larger farms will almost certainly emerge from the present regime of minifundia, but the nature of this further socio-economic revolution will be for the evolving civil society to determine in due course.

The way forward for large rural populations might best be seen in terms of further rural–urban migration, with a choice between the reinforcement of large cities and the stimulation of local centres provided by the existing small towns and a selection of the best-placed rural settlements. But, at the same time, developing agricultural skills in the countryside and presenting agriculture as a worthwhile career for young people would seem to be an economic necessity which is difficult to reconcile with the ambivalence of prevailing policies. And in view of the social importance of small farms there may be relevance in the 'Bavarian approach', through family farms linked with rewarding ancillary employment. A large rural population is a resource which entrepreneurially minded local authorities may exploit, in anticipation of spontaneous counter-urbanizing trends which may be reinforced in the years ahead. In this context local culture could be a particular asset in the context of community tourism.

In the Carpathians the 'best scenario' outlined above has not materialized and indeed has been shown to rest on an unrealistic appreciation of the transition. On the other hand, the 'worst scenario' has been averted through a major restitution programme and reconstruction of local government which is slowly providing a base for future growth and diversification. There is increasing population mobility to reduce rural isolation. In Romania, as in Eastern Europe, the mountain regions have reached different stages in the demographic transition. In some areas the human resources are badly depleted, while in others they remain substantial. So far, East European governments have been preoccupied with urban-industrial issues and rural policy has been dominated by restitution, which meets an immediate political need but does not address long-term issues. The issues of EU enlargement and the implications of the CAP, however, will direct increasing attention to rural areas in future.

References

Ben-Ner, A. and Montias, J. M. (1991), 'The Introduction of Markets in a Hypercentralised Economy: The Case of Romania', *Journal of Economic Perspectives*, vol. 5, pp. 163–70.

Bordanc, F. (1995), 'Spatial Variations in the Process of Agricultural Land Privatisation', in D. Turnock (ed.), *Rural Change in Romania*, Leicester University Geography Department, Occasional Paper 33, Leicester, pp. 39–47.

Briggs, D. (1993), 'Romania: On the Starting Blocks or Running out of Steam?', *Business Europa*, vol. 1, no. 5, pp. 7–17.

Caraiani, G. (1991), 'Zonele libere si dezvoltarea regionala', *Tribuna Economica*, vol. 2, no. 37, p. 7.
Cianga, N. (1991), 'Un model de cuantificare a potentialului si bazei materiale turistice din regiunea montana', *Studia Universitatis Babes-Bolyai: Geographia*, vol. 36, no. 1, pp. 105–8.
Davidovici, I. (1991), 'Strategia de restructare a agriculturii', *Tribuna Economica*, vol. 2, no. 37, p. 6.
Fiedler, H. (1992), *Innovation Centres in Central and Eastern Europe*, Berlin.
Florea, A. (1992), 'Restructurarea necesitate a eficientizarii industriei romanesti', *Tribuna Economica*, vol. 3, nos. 8–9, p. 3.
Fratila, G. (1992), 'Sint asociatiile agricole necesare?', *Tribuna Economica*, vol. 3, no. 6, pp. 25–6.
Golopentia, A. and Georgescu, D. C. (1942), *60 sate romanesti*, Institutul de Stiinte Sociale, Bucharest.
Guran, L. (1994), *Foreign Investments in Romania: A Geographic Survey*, Romanian Academy, Geography Institute, Bucharest.
Hoffman, O. (1991), 'Societatea civila si cea politica in procesul tranzitiei in Romania', *Sociologie Romaneasca*, vol. 2, pp. 137–46.
Hoffman, O. (1992), 'Problemele protectiei sociale in procesul tranzitiei in Romania', *Sociologie Romaneasca*, vol. 3, pp. 263–72.
Ianoş, I. (1995), 'The Romanian Village Advances towards a New State of Equilibrium', in D. Turnock (ed.), *Rural Change in Romania*, Leicester University Geography Department, Occasional Paper 33, Leicester, pp. 12–18.
Ianoş, I. et al. (1992), 'Changements recents dans l'agriculture roumaine', *Revue Roumaine: Geographie*, vol. 36, pp. 9–15.
Ianoş, I. and Talanga, C. (1994), *Orasul si sistemul urban romanesc in conditiile economiei de piata*, Academia Romana Institut de Geografie, Bucharest.
Iosif, G. N. (1991), 'Zootehnia romaneasca la ora adevarului', *Tribuna Economica*, vol. 2, no. 38, pp. 6–7.
Iosif, G. N. (1992), 'Necesitatea revitalizarii cooperativelor mestesugaresti', *Tribuna Economica*, vol. 3, no. 50, p. 13.
Iosif, G. N. (1994a), 'Dotarea tehnica a agriculturii: a prioritate absoluta', *Tribuna Economica*, vol. 5, no. 5, pp. 1–2; ibid., no. 6, p. 2.
Iosif, G. N. (1994b), 'Prezentul si perspectiva societatilor si asociatiilor din agricultura', *Tribuna Economica*, vol. 5, no. 19, pp. 13–14; ibid., no. 20, p. 11.
Iosif, G. N. (1994c), 'Restructurarea si privatizarea in zootehnie', *Tribuna Economica*, vol. 5, no. 21, p. 4.
Karp, L. and Stefanou, S. (1994), 'Domestic and Trade Policy for Central and East European Agriculture', *Economics of Transition*, vol. 2, pp. 345–71.
Kideckel, D. A. (1992), 'Peasants and Authority in the New Romania', in D. N. Nelson (ed.), *Romania after Tyranny*, Westview, Boulder, CO, pp. 67–81.
Kligman, G. (1990), 'Reclaiming the Public: A Reflection on Creating Civil Society in Romania', *East European Politics and Societies*, vol. 4, pp. 393–438.
Marsh, V. and Done, K. (1995), 'Romania: Reform Process at a Critical Juncture', *Financial Times*, 25 May, pp. 33–6.
Miron, M. (1991), 'Atragerea de capital strain in Romania prin zonele libere industriale', *Tribuna Economica*, vol. 2, no. 17, p. 11.
Mironiuc, M. (1994), 'Procesul decizional in exploatatile agricole familiale', *Tribuna Economica*, vol. 5, no. 17, pp. 10–12.

Muica, C. and Muica, N. (1995), 'Landcover Change and its Ecological Consequences', in D. Turnock (ed.), *Rural Change in Romania*, Leicester University Geography Department, Occasional Paper 33, Leicester, pp. 64–6.

Nicolaescu, N. (1993), 'Privatisation in Romania: The Case for Financial Institutions', in D. E. Fair and R. J. Raymond (eds), *The New Europe: Evolving Economic and Financial Systems in East and West*, Kluwer Publishers, Dordrecht, pp. 101–9.

Parpala, O. (1992a), 'Crearea de ferme agricole private viabile', *Tribuna Economica*, vol. 3, nos. 3–4, p. 25.

Parpala, O. (1992), 'Criza generala a agriculturii romanesti postdecembriste', *Tribuna Economica*, vol. 3. no. 27, p. 6; ibid., no. 29, p. 3; ibid., no. 31, p. 7; ibid., no. 32, p. 7; and ibid., no. 33, pp. 6–7.

Parpala, O. (1993), 'Politica structurilor forme asociative in agricultura', *Tribuna Economica*, vol. 4, no. 30, pp. 9–10.

Repassy, H. and Symes, D. (1993), 'Perspectives on Agrarian Reform in East Central Europe', *Sociologia Ruralis*, vol. 33, pp. 81–91.

Rey, R. (1979), *Viitor in Carpati: progres economic civilizatie socialism*, Scrisul Romanesc, Craiova.

Roper, S. D. (1994), 'The Romanian Revolution from a Theoretical Perspective', *Communist and Post-Communist Societies*, vol. 27, pp. 401–10.

Surd, V. (1991), 'Traditional Forms of Organizing Geographical Space in Transylvania: "The Lands"', *Studia Universitatis Babes-Bolyai: Geographia*, vol. 36, no. 2, pp. 74–80.

Surd, V. (1994), 'Critical Status of Rural Romania', in F. Grief (ed.), *Die Zukunft des landlichen Infrastruktur in Ostmitteleuropa*, Schriftenreihe der Bundesanstalt fur Agrarwirtschaft, 75, Vienna, pp. 61–7.

Talaba, I. (1991), *Turism in Carpatii Orientali*, Editura pentru Turism, Bucharest.

Talanga, C. (1995), 'The Restructuring of Industrial Activities in Romanian Villages', in D. Turnock (ed.), *Rural Change in Romania*, Leicester University Geography Department, Occasional Paper 33, Leicester, pp. 50–3.

Tismaneanu, V. (n.d.), *Understanding National Stalinism: A Comparative Approach to the History of Romanian Communism*, Smithsonian Institution Wilson Center East European Programme, Occasional Paper 25.

Turnock, D. (1992), *The Romanian Countryside at the End of State Socialism*, Leicester University Geography Department, Occasional Paper 22, Leicester.

Turnock, D. (1993), *Agricultural Change in the Romanian Carpathians*, University of Leicester Faculty of Social Sciences Discussion Papers in Geography, 93/2, Leicester.

Turnock, D. (1994), *Regional Development in the New Eastern Europe with Special Reference to Romania*, University of Leicester Faculty of Social Sciences Discussion Papers in Geography, G94/1, Leicester.

Turnock, D. (1995), 'The Rural Transition in Eastern Europe', *GeoJournal*, vol. 36, pp. 420–6.

Turnock, D. and Turnock, M. (1995), 'The Transition in Romania: The Perspective from Britain', in D. Turnock (ed.), *Rural Change in Romania*, Leicester University Geography Department, Occasional Paper 33, Leicester, pp. 1–11.

Zoican, I. (1992), 'Reorientari in domeniul agriculturii romanesti', *Tribuna Economica*, vol. 3, no. 2, pp. 4–5; ibid., no. 6, p. 4.

15 Albania, Macedonia and Bulgaria: A Belt of Opportunity and Instability

GEORGE PRÉVÉLAKIS

Albania, Macedonia and Bulgaria are three states with many things in common. They share their recent experience of Communism, their older heritage of nationalism and Balkanization, and the even older memories of the Ottomon Empire. In the context of the processes of change in East-Central Europe, economics, politics and culture converge to link together these three states in a special category.

Contrary to their neighbours in former Yugoslavia, they have managed until now to preserve peace in their territories. The end of the Cold War has opened an era of opportunity for the three states, but this optimistic perspective is darkened by the growing geopolitical tensions in their area.

The Opportunities

In a reunified European space, the geographical situation constitutes an important advantage. The territories of the three states are at the core of an enormous crossroads linking Europe, Asia and Africa: the Balkans. Many of the major axes of this crossroads span the space of Albania, Macedonia and Bulgaria. They are:

The Moravian–Vardar corridor

This corridor links the Danube with the Eastern Mediterranean. It has played an important role in the past and for this reason major cities have developed along its path: Belgrade, Skopje, Salonika. After the Balkan Wars this axis was divided between Serbia and Greece and at the beginning of the Cold War it was bisected by the Iron Curtain. The special status of Yugoslavia during the Cold War, however, and the advantages of the route itself have led to a relatively important circulation. The Yugoslav crisis, the embargo against Serbia and the Athens–Skopje dispute over the name of Macedonia have all contributed to the temporary neutralization of this axis. Macedonia's position on the Morava–Vardar corridor — between Greece and Serbia — gives her an important advantage, but is also a source of danger. In fact, the communications of Greece with the European Union by land, Serbia's line to the open sea (especially if she has difficulties of access to the Adriatic) and finally contact between Greece and Serbia, two countries with a tradition of co-operation, all depend on Skopje.

The Via Egnatia

The Via Egnatia follows a direction perpendicular to that of the Morava–Vardar corridor. It used to be a main route of the Roman Empire linking the 'First' Rome with the 'Second' (Constantinople), the Adriatic with the Black Sea. The Via Egnetia starts in Dyrrachium (Durrës, the port-city of Tirana) and continues through Albania, Macdeonia, Greece, the port of Salonica, and Greek and Turkish Thrace to arrive in Istanbul. This road is now almost abandoned, with the exception of certain parts of it (for example, from Salonica to the Greek border with Turkey).

The Via Imperialis

An important road in the Byzantine Empire, this axis used to link Constantinople with the Morava–Vardar corridor through important cities like Adrianopolis (Edirne) and Serdica (Sofia). Many invasions of Constantinople followed this axis.

The Turkish policy is to favour the development of a parallel to the Via Egnatia axis which would result from the combination of the western part of the Via Egnatia with the eastern part of the Via Imperialis. This route would pass through Turkish and Bulgarian Thrace (via Erdine) and then through Macedonia and Albania, arriving in Durrës. The advantage of such a new road for Turkey is that it would not traverse Greek territory.

The road linking the Black Sea with the Aegean Sea

Turkey has an important regional advantage in the control of the Bosporus, which gives her considerable leverage on all the countries surrounding the Black Sea (since their only valid sea route to the open sea is though the straits). The next most convenient way from the Black Sea to the Aegean Sea is through the territories of Bulgaria and Greece. Such a route could start at the Bulgarian port of Burgas on the Black Sea and end at the port of Porto-Lagos on the Aegean (between Alexandroupolis/Dedeagach). The development of this axis is associated with a scenario of Greek–Bulgarian co-operation (unfavourable to Turkey), which more or less denies the possibility of Turkish–Bulgarian co-operation (unfavourable to Greece) in the form of an axis parallel to the Via Egnatia. Bulgaria has two major geopolitical options to play with, and could possibly try to combine both.

By this brief analysis, it is possible to understand the importance from both an economic and geopolitical viewpoint of the axes passing through the territories of Albania, Macedonia and Bulgaria. The three countries thus have a series of substantial advantages that can be used for their economic development and in their relations both with each other and with their neighbours (Greece, Turkey and Serbia).

The historical experience of the populations which have lived in this crossroads region has enriched their cultures, and these cultures constitute an important asset in a world which is moving away from the economic model of the industrialized nation state. The tradition of living in a multicultural environment, the capacity for trade rather than industrial occupation among the city-dwellers, the ease with which the Balkan populations migrate and in general accept a life of spatial mobility — all these characteristics contribute to the ease with which they can adapt to the changing environment of a more and more tertiary-oriented and globalized world. A major expression of these cultural characteristics is the role of the Balkan diasporas, which have proved valuable to their mother countries in the context of the transition towards a market economy and a Western political system.

These three Balkan states have natural resources in addition to the asset of their human capital. Bulgaria has great agricultural potential. In Albania, there are important mineral resources, and the Albanian coast could be used for high-class tourism, especially if the Albanian authorities make use of the experience of Greece and former Yugoslavia in order to keep a balance between economic growth and environmental protection. Bulgaria also has an important potential for tourism along Black Sea coasts, a region easily accessible to the big markets of Eastern Europe.

The belt between the Adriatic and the Black Sea which makes up the territories of Albania, Macedonia and Bulgaria could become one of the most rapidly developing areas of the world in the context of European integraton, if it receives the necessary capital, assistance, know-how and encouragement from Europe. The growth of the Greek economy during the past decades is an example of these possibilities. In fact, the countries of the Adriatic/Black Sea belt could develop even faster than Greece during the past decades, since they start from a lower level and because of the new economic environment created by the end of the Cold War.

The Dangers

The necessary condition for development, however, is political stability. In this respect, the heritage of the Cold War is a heavy burden for the Balkans. Most of the pre-Second-World-War geopolitical problems have re-emerged in a renewed form and constitute a major threat to the peace of the region.

The Albanian Question

The territory of Albania does not cover the whole of the Albanian ethnic space. There are important Albanian communities in the Serbian territory of Kosovo and in western Macedonia. There is thus an Albanian irredentism which has become a major destabilizing factor. In the short term, the biggest danger seems to be in Macedonia, where military control is much less tight than in Kosovo. On the other hand, Albania is confronted on its own territory with a Greek Orthodox minority which is the source of much tension with its southern neighbour, Greece. For Greeks, southern Albania is in fact northern Epirus — the northern part of the Greek-populated region of Epirus.

The Macedonian Question

Macedonia has problems not only with Albania and its own Albanians, but also with Greece, Bulgaria and Serbia. According to Macedonians, there is a Macedonian Region, birthplace of the Macedonian nation, which was divided among three states — Greece, Serbia and Bulgaria — after the Balkan Wars. Only within Tito's Yugoslavia was the Macedonian nation able to live in relative independence which thus helped it to create a sovereign state after the Yugoslav crisis. In this Macedonian vision there is an irredentist element towards Greek Macedonia and Bulgarian Macedonia which may find its expression in the future in political or even terrorist activity. On the one hand, the Greeks consider Macedonia history (marked by heroes like Alexander the Great and Aristotle and so on) to be part of Greek history and refuse any non-Greek population the right to use the name of Macedonia. To oblige the Macedonians to change their name, they obstructed (more or less unsuccessfully) the recognition of the new state and imposed an embargo on all Macedonian imports and exports through Salonica. The Bulgarians consider that the Macedonians are in fact Bulgarians, since their language is close to Bulgarian, and claim that the state of Macedonia is nothing other than a second Bulgarian state which may one day be united with Bulgaria itself. Finally, the Serbs are interested in keeping open the road to Greece, which crosses Macedonian territory.

The Bulgarian Question

In addition to their implication in the Macedonian question, there are two other possible sources of tension between Bulgaria and her neighbours. On the one hand there is the problem of the Muslim minority in Bulgaria. As in Greek Thrace, the important Muslim minority in Bulgaria has developed a Turkish national identity over the years. During its latter period, the Bulgarian Communist regime evicted the larger part of this minority to Turkey, but most later returned. In the later political circumstances, their party played a crucial role in Bulgarian politics and pushed Bulgaria towards co-operation with Turkey and towards renunciation of the policy of the Athens–Sofia axis, which had been the result of the patient efforts of two former presidents, Zhivkov and Karamanlis. The second Bulgarian-related problem is the old dream of an exit to the Aegean Sea, which would offer Bulgaria (and its allies) total control of the land route from the Black Sea to the Mediterranean. This project would bring Bulgaria into conflict with both Greece and Turkey, but would be strongly supported by Russia.

This chain of problems and tensions ranging from the Adriatic to the Black Sea could lead to a general explosion, depending on various scenarios. One of these is based on the possibility of an outburst of the Albanian problem in Macedonia, which could lead to the dismemberment of Macedonia and the division of its territories between Albania and Bulgaria. In such a case, joint Greco-Serbian military action to secure a common border could not be excluded. What would be the reaction of Turkey under such circumstances? The possibility of a third Balkan war involving Greece and Serbia on the one hand and Albania, Bulgaria and Turkey on the other (Macedonia being simply transformed into an arena) cannot be dismissed.

The Role of Europe

Yugoslavia has already succombed to the demons of the past and at the moment there seems to be a continual threat of war in former Yugoslavia. Will the Adriatic/Black Sea belt follow its Yugoslav neighbour onto the path of self-destruction, engaging Greece and Turkey in a major adventure, or can we hope that the forces of disruption — which for the time being are developing more and more — will be counterbalanced by the logic of economic co-operation for the benefit of all? Much depends on the attitude of the international community towards the region, since the internal factors have in them both the good and the bad.

In fact, the Yugoslav crisis is the expression of deeper problems on the European scale. The end of the Cold War produced doubt as to the capacity or the will of any power to control the outbursts of violence in the most sensitive — from a geopolitical point of view — areas of Europe. In addition, the return of some old antagonisms in the West European sphere has led to what have appeared as hesitiations and doubts about the policy to follow in Yugoslavia. In their turn these hesitations have put more oil on the fire of former Yugoslavia. As the European crisis deepens (with the contradictory visions of Germany and Great Britain about Europe and the hesitations of France as expressed in presidential election debate, and so on), one can fear the worst for the Balkans. Europe is too preoccupied with its own problems to spend its energy on pacifying Yugoslavia. The European politicians express themselves about their capability to cope with the complicated Balkan issues with more and more pessimism and they tend to accept the 'destiny' of the Balkan people to slaughter each other with resignation. With the new Kosovo crisis in the south of the peninsula, Europe is finding itself in a far more difficult position than before in front of such a new humiliation in its 'back-yard'. For this reason, Europe should act now to divert the trends from the path of confrontation to the path of co-operation. It is difficult, however, to imagine Europe embarking today on a policy of anticipation of problems, immersed as she is in problems that she finds more and more difficult to handle.

If the internal political problems of Europe did not interfere with a rational geopolitical strategy at its periphery, it would not be too difficult to construct a policy aimed at preventing future conflicts in the Balkans. Such a policy would promote confidence in the future by supporting a number of ambitious trans-border regional development projects. The most obvious among them would be centred on the substantial development of the transport infrastructures of the Morava–Vardar corridor. In a more general way, the experiences of German unification could be profitably applied in the Balkans.

Although the present European situation inspires more pessimism than optimism, from a longer-term perspective it is not impossible to hope that the great natural and human advantages of the area from Albania to Bulgaria will lead to the progress and prosperity of the peoples that live in this southern belt of the Balkans. If Europe does not manage to speak at last, however, in a single and persuasive voice to the inhabitants of its 'soft underbelly' — as Churchill named the Balkan peninsula — the calm may come only after a storm of considerable intensity.

16 The Restructuring of Urban and Rural Settlement in Estonia: A Comment

TIM UNWIN

Introduction

Ann Marksoo's chapter provides a detailed overview of the development of urban and rural settlement systems, demographic change, employment structure and farm privazation in Estonia since the 1980s. This commentary shall explore some of the structural imperatives underlying these changes, and shall focus in particular on the implications of the adoption of capitalist relations of production in Estonia for urban–rural interaction. I shall argue, in essence, that the emphasis on adherence to the principles of a free market economy, as recommended by the World Bank and the IMF (Odling-Smee, 1992; World Bank, 1993), has led to increasing differentiation between rural and urban areas. As has long been argued (Lipton, 1977; Johnston, 1984; Harvey, 1985), one of the key characteristics of capitalism has been its tendency to create increased inequalities between these two kinds of place (Potter and Unwin, 1995), and this chapter seeks to draw attention to some of the potential future implications of such transformations. Its core arguments are summarized in Figure 16.1, which draws attention to four main processes: the creation of place (see also Unwin, 1992); the role of planning controls; the interests of foreign capital; and urban–rural interaction (see Potter and Unwin, 1989).

The Restructuring of Urban and Rural Settlement in Estonia

Six key empirical themes can be developed from Marksoo's chapter on recent changes in urban and rural settlements in Estonia: the underlying cultural significance of rural areas; the connectivity of urban and rural employment; the enduring environmental significance of Russian military occupation; the linkages between land reform and farm reform; the need for an integrated rural development policy; and the inherited structure of industrial development.

Rural Areas in Estonia's Cultural Heritage

The emergence of an independent Estonian state following the end of the First World War was intimately tied up with the creation of a particular national identity, one of whose key characteristics was a specific emphasis on rural culture and lifestyles. The Land Reform Law of 1919 led to the redistribution of 2,346,494 hectares of land and the creation of 83,514 independent holdings (Pullerits, 1937). The subsequent emergence of an agrarian economy based on small privately held farms (Aunap and Mander, 1991; Abrahams and Kahk, 1994), the reclamation of land and the development of a successful dairy industry all helped to reinforce an Estonian identity in which rural images (in the ideological sphere) and activities (in the economic sphere) played a critical part. With the annexation of Estonia by Russia during the Second World War, the subsequent nationalization of land and the creation of state and collective farms, the 'rural' took on a new kind of meaning. Two aspects of this meaning, in particular, can be noted. First, many Estonians fled to the forests in order to escape Russian persecution. Indeed, some people lived secret lives, hidden away in cellars beneath forest farms, for a considerable period of the early Russian occupation. Here the 'rural' took on an identity of opposition and escape. Secondly, though, despite the urbanization that occurred throughout the Soviet period, many Estonians retained an interest in the countryside, maintaining rural cottages to which they could travel for holidays or at weekends. Once again, therefore, the rural maintained a particular significance and meaning, even for urban dwellers. With the arrival of Estonia's second period of independence in the 1990s, these underlying cultural factors have re-emerged as being highly significant in the shaping of a new Estonian identity, in which rural images and practices retain an important role.

The Connectivity between Urban and Rural Employment

Marksoo has drawn attention to the highly significant linkage between urban and rural employment. She thus highlights the critical need for the enhancement of rural employment possibilities in order to prevent massive future migration from rural areas to the cities of Tallinn and Tartu. The current restructuring and contraction of industry in the main urban centres of Estonia means that there are insufficient urban employment opportunities in the short term should such migration take place. There is therefore considerable potential for political unrest resulting from economic dissatisfaction, particularly from the growing number of young people entering the employment market. A critical issue at stake here is whether or not the structural economic adjustments set in motion following the recommendations of the World Bank and the IMF will in the end generate sufficient urban employment to absorb such migration (Lugus and Hacey, 1995). Experience from the Third World suggests that this is unlikely to be the case, at least in the short term (Potter and Unwin, 1989, 1995).

The Enduring Environmental Significance of Russian Military Occupation

A third sigificant issue to emerge since 1990 has been the environmental influence of half a century of Russian military occupation. Thus large areas of rural Estonia were taken over for military use as training grounds, airfields, missile bases or naval harbours. Two particular implications of this are pertinent to the present discussion. First, where such installations have been built, the nature of the physical environment has been transformed to such an extent that in most instances it is not possible for people who lay claim to the land to use it for agricultural purposes. Put quite simply, it is not easy to convert runways and missile silos into fields. Secondly, though, there has been substantial pollution resulting from the military use of rural areas. Groundwater resources have been damaged through the release of fuel into underground aquifiers, there are dumps of shells and mines which require careful reclamation, and the nuclear reactor at the former submarine base of Paldiski still requires dismantling.

Distinctions between Land Reform and Farm Reform

As Marksoo illustrates, one of the key factors influencing the settlement structure of Estonia since the late 1980s has been the development of private farms and the introduction of land reform legislation (see also Abrahams and Kahk, 1994; Unwin, 1994a, 1994b; Maide, 1995). Central to an understanding of this development is the recognition that the two processes have been largely separate, and that they have taken place in a vacuum of agrarian policy. While those who can show rights to land dating back to the 1930s are in general able to claim these rights, this process of land privatization has been largely divorced from that determining the future of the former state and collective farms. Indeed, the considerable uncertainty that exists over the viability of Estonian agriculture in the context of the global economy means that many of the workers formerly involved in the farming sector have little incentive to remain therein. Furthermore, by basing the process of land privatization on the landholding structure that existed in the 1930s, new land holdings are being created that will effectively not be viable as agricultural enterprises.

The Need for an Integrated Rural Development Policy

In the light of the above comments, there is a critical need for the Estonian government to establish an integrated rural development policy which will seek to provide rural employment possibilities for the considerable numbers of rural people who will become unemployed through the restructuring of agricultural enterprises and the process of land reform (Unwin, 1994b). As Marksoo has shown, approximately one quarter of the employed population of Estonia is still to be found in rural areas, and given the limited extent of urban industrial employment opportunities available to them it is essential that they are provided with a sound economic base for their survival.

The Inherited Industrial Base

Estonia was formerly one of the most advanced of the Soviet Republics (Von Arkadie and Karlsson, 1993; Bradshaw, 1991). Its industrial structure, however, was geared largely to the production of energy and a range of industrial goods, including armaments, which have become redundant following the country's separation from the former Soviet Union. Much of the labour required by this industrial base was provided for through the immigration of Russians, who at the time of independence were ethnically in the majority in Tallinn and the north-eastern cities of Narva, Sillamäe and Kohtla-Järva. The position of this substantial Russian population is still one of great political sensitivity, and it is unlikely to be resolved until the government has been able to develop a sound new economic base for the country. This it has chosen to do through the path of widespread privatization and the rapid introduction of a market economy (Lugus and Hachey, 1995). It is therefore appropriate now to explore some of the underlying factors which have brought this about, and their likely influence on the future development of Estonia.

The Broader Agenda

For an all too brief window of opportunity during the late 1980s and early 1990s, there was an exciting possibility that the newly independent countries of Eastern Europe and the former Soviet Union might be able to tread a delicate path between the two contrasting economic models of capitalism and Communism; in short, that they might be able to identify a third way. As Habermas (1990; see also 1994) has so clearly identified, though, capitalism has shown a remarkable ability to undermine supposedly post-capitalist as well as pre-capitalist social formations (Potter and Unwin, 1995). An analysis of the precise means by which this has happened lies well beyond the remit of this commentary, but Figure 16.1 seeks to draw attention to some of the key processes that are currently taking place in the transformation of the Estonian economy.

Ideology and the Creation of Place

The meaning of place is highly contentionus and complex (see Massey, 1994), but for the present purposes places can be interpreted as the creations of particular peoples and societies through their interaction both with and within a specific physical environment (Unwin, 1992). Thus Figure 16.1 represents the way in which new places are created through the operation of a particular economy (the capitalist market economy) in and through a past place. Such places have many characteristics, but in the context of Marksoo's chapter it seems pertinent to draw attention to three aspects of them, namely their agriculture, housing and industry.

Central to understanding the transformations currently under way in Estonia, as elsewhere in much of Eastern Europe, is a distinction to be made in the terminology used to describe the type of economic transformation aspired to. Thus, rather than the term capitalism, two distinct phrases have been used in the rhetoric associated with economic and political transformation of the country: the free market economy and democracy. Economic policies introduced by governments since independence have had at their core the introduction of mechanisms designed to replace the central command economy with conditions which permit the operation of a so-called free market. Privatization of the means of production and the introduction of macro-economic financial policy instruments have been crucial policy instruments in achieving these ends.

It is important, however, to recognize the key role that ideology has played in these developments. In particular, the conjunction of the political concept of democracy with the economic idea of a free market economy has played a powerful role in the changes that have taken place. The aspiration of the mass of the people was for political independence from the former Soviet Union, and thus for democracy, a concept seen as providing a greater degree of individual freedom than had theretofore been experienced by the majority of the population.

Figure 16.1 The capitalist market economy and 'place'

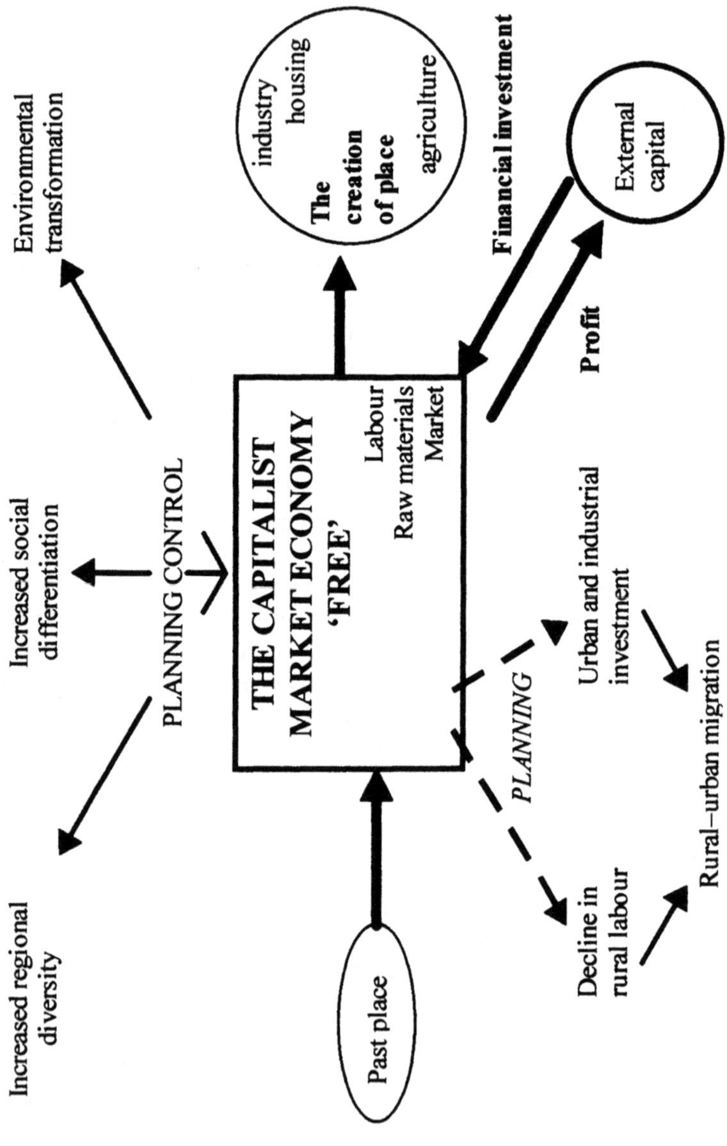

The economic reality of this, though, was an adherence to a policy creating a market economy, in which individual market forces are free to determine the overall structure of the economy. It is these forces that are creating the place of contemporary Estonia, through their influence in such empirical realities as the country's industry, agriculture and housing. Any recognition that the market economy is free only to those with power to benefit from it, or that democracy in reality only serves those in power, has been ignored or deliberately swept under the carpet.

Planning and Place in Estonia

Figure 16.1 indicates two particular ways in which planning can influence the reality of places under capitalism. The upper part of Figure 16.1 illustrates that the capitalist market economy has three particular tendencies: increased social differentiation; increased regional diversity; and environmental transformation. The introduction of planning controls can limit the adverse effects of these to some extent, through the implementation of differential taxation regimes and regional reallocations of budgetary expenditure. As yet within Estonia there is little sign of this happening with regard to the first two tendencies, but it is interesting to note that substantial efforts have already been made to introduce appropriate environmental legislation (see, for example, Environmental Data Centre, 1992, 1993). In part this reflects a desire to overcome the serious environmental degradation under the former Soviet regime, but it is also one positive aspect of the potential for future change in Estonia.

A second way in which planning policies can serve to ameliorate the adverse effects of the capitalist mode of production is through their role in influencing urban–rural linkages (Potter and Unwin, 1989). It is widely accepted that capitalist economies have generally emerged through a sequence of change involving a decline in rural population and employment, and a commensurate increase in urban settlement and employment (Johnston, 1984). It is these changes to which Marksoo alludes in her chapter. Within Estonia, however, given the particular importance of its rural cultural heritage, it is appropriate to ask whether this is indeed the most appropriate path for the state's future development. Given the aspirations of many Estonian citizens to reclaim their rural land and for there to be a viable agrarian sector, it can be argued that serious attempts should be made to develop a comprehensive integrated rural development policy associated with the new regional policy to which Marksoo refers in her conclusion.

The Interests of Foreign Capital

The final part of Figure 16.1 reflects the role of external capital. A comprehensive account of the role of foreign capital in Estonia since independence remains to be written, but it is evident that it has largely been drawn to relatively few sectors of the economy and that little has been attracted to rural areas. Moreover, the level of foreign investment has often been lower than that desired by many Estonians. This reflects at least two factors: the perceived insecurity of financial investment in Estonia and the much higher immediate returns on such investment in the major growth economies of the world.

Nevertheless, it is salient to note that foreign capital is fundamentally interested in ensuring that profits are greater than the financial investment, illustrated by the differential in arrow sizes in Figure 16.1. As such, its main concerns are with the identification and exploitation of, on the one hand, cheap labour, power and raw materials and, on the other, of an expanded market. It is precisely the conditions through which these can be achieved that the IMF and the World Bank have sought to facilitate through macroeconomic recommendations concerning changes to such things as fiscal and monetary policy.

Conclusions

Marksoo's chapter has drawn attention to the empirical detail of urban and rural settlement change in Estonia since independence. This commentary has sought to explore some of the structural changes and tendencies underlying such empirical realities. It is these that go to make up the many different places of Estonia. At the heart of capitalism is a concern with difference, exploitation and individual profit. The only freedom of the market economy is the freedom enjoyed by those who can benefit from it. If the dramatic changes that have taken place in the former Soviet Union and Eastern Europe over recent years are going to be of lasting benefit to those who strove for individual freedom under the banner of democracy, then governments such as that of Estonia must grapple with some of the complex issues of regional planning policy to which Marksoo alludes. The opportunity of a third way has long since passed; Estonia is well and truly entrapped in the complex web of capitalism. Nevertheless, and particularly in such a small country as Estonia, the chance still remains for the introduction of comprehensive place-sensitive policies which will ameliorate the excessive differential influences of the capitalist market economy.

Acknowledgements

Funding from the British Academy, the Estonian Academy of Sciences and the European Union for research upon which this commentary is based is gratefully acknowledged, as is advice and assistance from Anton Laur and Reet Karukäpp.

References

Abrahams, R. and Kahk, J. (1994), *Barons and Farmers: Continuity and Transformation in Rural Estonia (1816–1994)*, University of Göteborg, Göteborg.

Aunap, R. and Mander, Ü. (1991), 'Estonian Agriculture', in K. Sepp (ed.), *European Workshop on Human Impact and Environment: North-East Estonia, Uusküla*, Tallinn, pp. 73–80.

Bradshaw, M. (ed.) (1991), *The Soviet Union: A New Regional Geography*, London.

Environmental Data Centre (1992), *Estonian Environment 1991*, Environment Data Centre, National Board of Waters and the Environment, Helsinki.

Environmental Data Centre (1993), *Estonian Environment 1992*, Environment Data Centre, National Board of Waters and the Environment, Helsinki.

Habermas, J. (1990), 'What Does Socialism Mean Today? The Rectifying Revolution and the Need for New Thinking on the Left', *New Left Review*, no. 183, pp. 3–21.

Habermas, J. (1994) (interviewed by M. Haller), *The Past as Future*, Cambridge.

Harvey, D. (1985), *City and Society: An Outline for Urban Geography*, London.

Lipton, M. (1977), *Why Poor People Stay Poor: A Study of Urban Bias in World Development*, London.

Lugus, O. and Hachey, G. A. Jr (eds) (1995), *Transforming the Estonian Economy*, Tallinn.

Maide, H. (1995), 'Transformation of Agriculture', in O. Lugus and G. A. Hachey Jr (eds), *Transforming the Estonian Economy*, Tallinn, pp. 169–86.

Massey, D. (1994), *Space, Place and Gender*, Cambridge.

Odling-Smee, J. (ed.) (1992), *Economic Review: Estonia*, IMF, Washington, DC.

Potter, R. B. and Unwin, T. (eds) (1989), *The Geography of Urban–Rural Interaction in Developing Countries*, London.

Potter, R. B. and Unwin, T. (1995), 'Urban–Rural Interaction: Physical Form and Political Process in the Third World', in *Cities* [IN PRESS: CHECK]

Pullerits, A. (ed.) (1937), *Estonia: Population, Culture and Economic Life*, Tallinn.

Unwin, T. (1992), *The Place of Geography*, Harlow.

Unwin, T. (1994a), 'Structural Change in Estonian Agriculture: From Command Economy to Privatisation', *Geography*, vol. 79, no. 3, pp. 246–61.

Unwin, T. (1994b), 'Agrarian Change and Integrated Rural Development in a Policy Vacuum', *European Urban and Regional Studies*, vol. 1, no. 2, pp. 180–5.

Van Arkadie, B. and Karlsson, M. (1992), *Economic Survey of the Baltic States: The Reform Process in Estonia, Latvia and Lithuania*, London.

World Bank (1993), *Estonia: The Transition to a Market Economy*, World Bank, Washington, DC.

17 Regional Change in Russia: New Scales, New Issues, New Actors[1]

M. J. BRADSHAW

Introduction

It is clear that the dramatic changes that have taken place in the former Soviet Union have made regions and regional issues far more important than they were during the Soviet era. This chapter explores the reasons for this growing interest in Russia's regions. At the heart of this exploration is the recognition that the collapse of the Soviet Union has led to both an erosion of central control, in the form of the Federal Government in Moscow, and an increase in the relative autonomy of local administrations in the eighty-nine federal subjects that make up the Russian Federation. Thus, the interest in Russia's regions reflects a major reconfiguration of the location of control and decision-making in Russia.

New Scales: Centralization and Decentralization

To understand the contemporary problems facing Russia's regions, it is necessary to consider the process of regional development during the Soviet period, although this is something of a misnomer. With the notable exception of the 'Sovnarkhoz' reforms during the Khrushchev period, the Soviet economy was not developed on a regional basis. Gosplan's Five Year Plans were drawn up on sectoral lines, that is by major industrial sector, rather than by republic or economic region. While it is true that the plan statements did contain sections that described development in individual republics and economic regions, these sections were little more than a summation of sectoral plans in a particular region, and not a coherent, integrated plan for the economic development in that particular region. Consequently, the regional priorities suggested by the plan statements, such as the move eastward in Siberia during the 1970s, were not the result of an explicit regional policy to develop Siberia, but rather the geographical consequence of the sectoral priorities.

The key points are: first, that the Soviet economy was not developed on a regional basis; and secondly, as a consequence of the nature of the economic system, that the dominant relationship was between the enterprise and its industrial ministry. Thus, individual enterprises in a particular region were vertically integrated into a ministerial system of control and their formal (horizontal) links to the local economy were marginal.[2] This resulted in high levels of regional interdependence as ministries sought to internalize their own linkages, rather than seek local sources of supply from enterprises subordinate to other ministries. In many instance towns were an amalgam of industry settlements each answerable to its own ministry in Moscow. For example, the city of Surgut in western Siberia was comprised of an 'oil town', a 'gas town' and a 'geology town'.

Under the Soviet central planning system the structure and pattern of economic development in a particular republic or region was the result of centralized decisions taken on a sectoral basis. While republican and local administrations could lobby the central authorities, they had very limited influence over the key decisions about the location of industrial activity on their territory. Thus, when the Soviet system collapsed, the newly independent republics and their composite regions inherited economic structures that were not of their making. Their failure to understand the high levels of regional interdependence created by the Soviet system led to the collapse of inter-republican and inter-regional trade.

The process of decentralization was at the heart of the reforms introduced by Mikhail Gorbachev under the banner of perestroika. The republican governments, particularly those in the Baltic states, seized the opportunity and decentralization soon gave way to disintegration. Within the Russian Federation Boris Yeltsin offered regional authorities greater autonomy to undermine Gorbachev's authority. In an attempt to counter these disintegrative tendencies, Gorbachev sought to reconfigure relations between the centre and the republics in the form of a new 'Federation Treaty'. It was on the eve of the signing of this treaty that conservative factions in Moscow launched the ill-fated coup that heralded the end of the Soviet Union. Having shed the mantle of the Soviet Union, Boris Yeltsin, now President of an independent Russian Federation, soon came to regret the promise he had made about giving Russia's regions greater authority. Institutional reforms implemented in Moscow served to dismantle the central planning system that had previously controlled the Russian economy; at the same time economic reforms were introduced that changed the position of the enterprise in the Russian economy. Not only did the centre surrender control, regional administration took the initiative and seized control of local assets. Thus, the division of ownership and responsibility between the Federal authorities in Moscow and local administrations (oblast-level and city-level) became, and remains, a key dimension of systemic transformation in Russia.

Administrations at the local level now have a degree of control that was unheard of during the Soviet period. Oblast-level administrations have devised their own tax structures and are now in the process of signing agreements with Federal government over the ownership of state-owned property and the division of tax revenues. Early on in this process local administrations found themselves having to take responsibility for much of the welfare structures — housing, schools and hospitals — that had previously been the responsibility of the large state-owned enterprises that dominated their local economies. Faced with increased responsibilities and a dwindling tax base, the local administrations could do little else than lobby Moscow for more funds and for a greater share of the tax revenue generated locally. Thus, the issue of 'fiscal federalism' and the division of revenues between the centre and the regions, and between rich and poor regions, remains at the centre of the political agenda in Russia today.

Dramatic changes have also taken place at the enterprise level. The collapse of the central planning system and the reconfiguration of the ministerial system served to isolate state-owned enterprises from the political decision-making process. Enterprise managers have had to look to opportunities in the local economy to ensure their survival. Increasing transportation costs have served to enhance this process of fragmentation as Russia's economic space has become a series of regional economies. In a very real sense the friction of distance has increased as the cost of moving goods has escalated. The privatization process has served to complete the severance of state-owned enterprises from benefactors in Moscow. Enterprise managers, now answerable to their shareholders, have focused on core activities, abandoning their social infrastructure to the local administration, and have sought to retain their workforces at all cost. This has been made possible by continued state subsidy as the Federal Government has made good inter-enterprise debt and has provided funds to pay wage arrears. The Federal Government can no longer afford such handouts, however, and bankruptcies and unemployment are on the increase. But there are also signs of new relations between enterprises in the regions and institutions in Moscow. Two recent developments suggest that the dominance of Moscow's banks is beginning to exert a new form of external control in Russia's regions. First, the recent 'shares for loans' programme introduced by the Federal Government, whereby commercial banks lent money to the government in return for the government's shares in state-owned enterprises, has prompted an angry reaction in the regions. In a number of cases the local enterprises have refused to acknowledge the commercial bank's ownership of these shares. Local administration are also wary of their key region-forming enterprises (huge industrial complexes that dominate the local economy) falling under the control of financial institutions in Moscow. Secondly, the emergence of 'Financial-Industrial Groups' (FIGs), which tie banks and enterprises together in a form of conglomerate, is also creating new patterns of inter-regional linkage and control. Again, Moscow financial dominance may be exerted through these FIGs as the key financial decisions are likely to be made in Moscow boardrooms. Thus, there is the possibility of Moscow's monopoly over the plan being replaced by control over access to capital markets.

In concluding this discussion on new scales, I want to suggest that the last decade has seen a reconfiguration of the location of decision-making in the Russian economy: first, through the policies of perestroika; and secondly, by the implementation of democratic and market-oriented reforms in the newly independent Russian Federation. Today it is possible to see different types of decision-making taking place at different levels in the Russia economy, whereas in the past all the important decisions were made at the centre. At the level of the national economy, the Federal Government is responsible for macroeconomic policy; at the regional level local administrations are capable of influencing the local economic environment through control over the local tax regime and the implementation of price control and other forms of local subsidy; at the enterprise level managers are now responsible for economic performance (rather than plan fulfilment) and have to take on the task of restructuring in the face of changes in ownership and the new commercial environment, as well as increasing foreign competition. Clearly there are complex lobbying processes at the local, regional and national level. Individual regional administrations may lobby for subsidies or for the implementation of industrial and regional policies that will benefit their region. Similarly, industry lobbies may campaign for greater protection from import-competition or for greater government support for their particular activity. Russia's regions are rapidly realizing that they are in competition with each other for the attention of the Federal Government and also for investment, both from domestic financial institutions and foreign investors. Some regions, such as the city of Nizhnii Novgorod, have been particularly successful in projecting an image as a go-ahead region. All this is a long way away from the system that created the Russian economy and it is at the regional level that the transformation of Russia is taking place. As a word of warning, however, it is dangerous to see the 'regions' themselves as the key economic actors in this process. True, individual administrations and regional governors can, and do, exert great influence over the local economic environment; it is individual enterprises and entrepreneurs, however, that actually make the economy work. Thus, in the Soviet system the making of regions was a highly centralized process; now the processes that make regions are taking place within the regions themselves. This challenges us to develop new ways of thinking about regional change in Russia.

New Issues: Monitoring Regional Change

Given what I have just said about the shift to the regional scale, it comes as no surprise that there is interest in assessing the regional dimensions of economic transition in Russia. It is apparent that the costs and benefits of economic change in Russia are generating clear 'winners and losers'. Some regions are benefiting from the current chaotic situation in Russia, while others are clearly suffering. The geography of winners and losers is also of political significance, as there is a growing relationship between the economic fortunes of particular regions and the political attitude of their inhabits. It is no surprise that the major commercial centres and resource-exporting regions have voiced their support for the reform parties. At the same time, the depressed agricultural regions and the old industrial regions have supported the resurgent Communist Party.

Not surprisingly, Western companies and the international lending agencies seem most interested in identifying and then supporting the winner regions. This is because they perceive them as relatively low risk locations in a high risk country, and because by supporting the success stories they believe they can promote the benefits of a market-type economy. Thus, institutions like the World Bank and the EBRD seem to help the regions and industries that need the least help, those that seem the most able to help themselves. The loser regions present a problem because they are also politically conservative and are proving themselves resistant to the imposition of market-type reforms. To confuse matters, there are also winner regions, such as Belgorod, that are conservative. The whole process of identifying winners and losers, however, is fraught with danger, added to which there is no guarantee that the regions currently doing well will remain competitive in a future market economy. In fact there are already signs that, due to the strengthening of the rouble and increasing production costs, some of the resource-producing regions have already lost their competitive advantage.

Assessment of the development trajectories of Russia's regions should be based on an understanding of the processes of economic restructuring now underway; rather than simply upon an assemblage of unreliable statistics. Ideally, a conceptual understanding of the processes shaping regional change should enable one to develop a more critical framework for statistical analysis of economic performance across Russia's regions. In monitoring regional change I find it useful to think of change as the interaction of two dynamics: 'the decline of the old' and 'the growth of the new'.

'The decline of the old' refers to the collapse of the industrial system created by the Soviet central planning system. The Soviet economy was hyper-industrialized with an emphasis on energy- and materials-intensive heavy industry, much of which was oriented toward the needs of the military-industrial complex. The lack of effective competitive pressures and the failure of the domestic innovation processes also meant that much of the capital stock was inefficient and antiquated. Thus, a large part of Russia's industrial base is not competitive in an international sense. Therefore, the 'transitional recession' that has accompanied Russia's transition to the market is not necessarily a bad thing. Much of the industrial production that has been lost was at best inefficient and in many instances unnecessary. The deindustrialization of the Russian economy, as well as the demilitarization of industry, is resulting in a downsizing of the industrial economy. So far the high levels of production decline (which are probably not as high as the official statistics suggest) has not resulted in excessive levels of unemployment or widespread bankruptcies. That this is the case has more to do with politics than economics. The Russian Government has been subsidizing state-owned and previously state-owned enterprises to keep unemployment at a politically acceptable level. This is in large part because Russia has gone through a lot of elections in a relatively short period of time. Once the Presidential elections have past, and should the international lending agencies pay close attention to what happens to their loans, then the Federal Government will stop supporting loss-making enterprises. Of course, perhaps with some justification, they could claim that they have staved off large-scale unemployment until now so that those who lose their jobs because of the decline of the old industries will find new jobs in new industries. This assumes, first, that the new jobs are in industry, and secondly, that the new jobs will be created in the regions that are likely to suffer the highest levels of unemployment. The experience of industrial restructuring in Western Europe and North America suggests that neither of these assumptions is likely to be the case. Equally, the collapse of the industrial economy in the Russian north and current high levels of out-migration are evidence that many old (in the sense that they were supported by the Soviet system) industrial regions will end up redundant spaces and that their populations will have to move to find new opportunities. The current shortage of housing and the relative absence of a housing market may mean that many people find themselves 'spatially entrapped' in single-industry towns whose industries have closed.

'The growth of the new' refers to new forms of economic activity that are emerging in Russia's fledgling market economy. In this context, the privatization process can be seen as something of a double-edged sword. Russia's state-owned enterprises were privatized ahead of restructuring. Thus, a change in ownership status is no guarantee of the future prosperity of an enterprise. Financing post-privatization restructuring is without doubt the key challenge facing previously state-owned enterprises. Enterprises producing the wrong product or finding themselves located in the wrong place will struggle to survive. Thus, many of them will be the final victims of the decline of the old system. It is the creation of new forms of economic activity that is likely to be the most important process. In some instances this may be a spin-off from a previously-owned state enterprise, in others it may be due to new entrepreneurial activity. Here foreign investors clearly have a role to play, although there may be a concern that foreign competition could kill off indigenous entrepreneurial activity. Obviously the previously state-owned enterprises are likely to dominate the major industrial sectors of the economy; it is the service sector, however, rather than industry, that is likely to generate economic growth and new employment. Entry costs are much lower in the service sector, as witnessed by the very rapid growth of private banks in Russia. This tertiarization of the Russian economy will benefit certain regions more than others. Already a set of regional financial centres are beginning to emerge and these same centres are proving to be the favoured locations for foreign investors. Thus cities such as St Petersburg, Nizhnii Novgorod, Samara, Ekaterinburg, Novosibirsk and Vladivostok are emerging as new growth centres. None of them is likely to challenge the dominance of Moscow, but they will serve as poles of attraction in the new Russian economy. In many instances these new centres are maintaining a dominance established during the Soviet period. It is, of course, possible that new centres of growth will emerge, but as yet it is unclear where they might be. For example, there may be the possibility of the Russian south emerging as a new 'sun-belt' region, but the deep conservatism of the region may hinder it from realizing its potential.

The problem regions for Russia are those that are suffering disproportionately from the decline of the old, but that show few signs of being in a position to benefit from the growth of the new. Quite where those regions are is difficult to determine. This is because the statistical system is far better at capturing the decline of the old Soviet economy than it is at monitoring the growth of new forms of economic activity. A major reason for this is that the new private sector is actively avoiding being enumerated because official registration would also mean having to pay taxes. There is also a deep-seated belief that only industrial activity counts, thus the statistical system is not designed to deal with the rapidly growing service economy. What this suggests is that we don't have a clear picture of the relative economic performance of Russia's regions.

New Actors

My earlier discussion of regional change focused on the changing power relations between the Federal Government and regional administrations. The transformation of the Russian economy has introduced two new sets of economic actors with an interest in Russia's regions: Moscow-based financial institutions and foreign financial institutions.

The Moscow-based financial institutions now have a clear interest in understanding what is happening in the regions. Many banks are either acquiring regional banks or setting up their own system of regional branches. At the same time the privatization process has left many banks and investment funds with major shareholdings in key region-forming enterprises. Thus, the attitudes of these powerful shareholders can influence the fortunes of individual regions and localities. As already mentioned, the shares-for-loans scheme and the emergence of FIGs has also resulted in Moscow-based financial institutions taking a greater interest in key enterprises in the regions. These new shareholders are already exerting their influence as they wish to see their interests protected. One of the supposed benefits for enterprises involved in FIGs is that they are thus provided with access to capital which they would be unlikely to be able to generate locally. Thus, it is increasingly the case that there are substantial regional variations in access to capital investment. This can only serve to amplify the increasing regional inequalities that are emerging in Russia. As yet, the Federal Government has not introduced a coherent regional development programme to support economic restructuring in regions unable to finance their own restructuring. Of course, in the West there is a clear ideological divide between governments that do and do not believe in the effectiveness of such regional policy. Given what has already been said about the geography of winners and losers, however, severely depressed regions are bound to emerge in Russia and such regions will attract the attention of the Federal Government. This is already the case with special programmes for the Russian north.

Foreign-based economic interests are best divided into private companies and international lending agencies, both of whom have an impact on economic development at the regional scale. It is now widely recognized that any company seeking to do business in Russia must travel beyond Moscow. In fact there are now companies who consciously decide to bypass Moscow and head straight to the regions. The decentralization of political control means that agreements must be reached with both the Federal Government and the regional administrations, as well as in many instances the municipal governments. Thus, would-be investors need to be able to gauge local attitudes toward foreign investors. A key indicator here is the regional distribution of foreign investment to date.

Clearly, a company's interest in Russia's regions is shaped by its motivations for entering the Russian market. It is possible to identify at least three main motivations: first, Russia as a market in which to sell products; secondly, Russia as a place to produce and obtain products; and thirdly, monitoring Russia as a source of potential competition. The initial phase of foreign investment in Russia was aimed at 'getting a foot in the door'. Operations were small-scale and mainly aimed at allowing the sale of products imported from outside. In the resource sector relatively small-scale projects aimed to enhance the efficiency of existing capacity. As Russia's reforms have progressed, however, sales have increased and investor confidence has grown, so much so that investors, particularly in the food and drink sectors (who produce a low-value bulk product with relatively low entry costs), are now setting up local production and extending their distribution networks beyond the immediate confines of Moscow and St Petersburg. Foreign companies are now asking the question: where next in Russia? Prior to this Moscow and St Petersburg had provided sufficient market for their small-scale operations. Now foreign companies need to monitor the political attitudes of Russia's regions, they need to evaluate the level of infrastructure development and assess the relative purchasing power of regional markets. The process of market penetration is made easier by the fact that most of Russia's population is located west of the Urals and that most people live in towns. The poor transportation system, however, makes access to markets beyond the regional centres problematic. In the resource-producing regions foreign investors are considering large-scale projects to develop new production capacity; here their reluctance to commit is due to problems with federal legislation as much as with local attitudes. Some regions remain openly hostile towards outside investors, be they from Moscow or New York.

At the same time as foreign investors have recognized that their future in Russia is tied to operating at the regional level, so the international financial institutions, such as the EBRD and the World Bank, have now recognized the need to target their support at particular regions. The question is then: which regions? The EBRD has set up a series of Regional Venture Capital Funds across Russia to support small and medium-sized enterprises. Support is also being provided to develop local financial institutions. The ILAs would do well to assess the regional impact of the assistance they have so far provided, however, before targeting regions through an explicit regional strategy. The EBRD's recent decision to target Moscow is symptomatic of a policy to support the winners rather than help the potential losers. This is to be expected given that the EBRD has to make a profit. However, perhaps the more humanitarian mandate of the World Bank will enable it to support Russia's problem regions.

Conclusions: New Scales, New Issues, New Actors

The central message of this chapter has been that this new interest in Russia's regions is because the current economic transformation in Russia is being orchestrated at the regional scale. Not only that, the processes of economic restructuring are generating winner and loser regions and the geography of growth and decline is unlikely to coincide. The result is growing levels of regional inequality and the emergence of economically depressed regions. In the European Union the process of integration has recognized the need for a 'coherence fund' to reduce level of regional inequality; in Russia it is clear that the growing level of inequality between regions promotes political instability. Finally, the processes of change at the local scale also involve new actors: local entrepreneurs and politicians, Moscow-based financiers and foreign investors and lending agencies. Thus, regional change in Russia, previously the geographical outcome of sectoral plans devised in Moscow, is now the result of a very complicated set of relationships stretching from the local to the global.

Notes

1 This paper was first published in L. B. Wallin (ed.), *Papers Presented to a Round-Table on Interest Groups on Russian Politics*, The Swedish National Defence Research Establishment, Stockholm, 1996, pp. 23–32.

2 Of course the 'unofficial' reality was somewhat different as enterprises had to develop their own local networks to compensate for the failings of the centrally planned economy. In addition, local party structures also provided a network for enterprise managers as party loyalty transcended the departmental boundaries of the industrial ministries.

References

Bradshaw, M. J. (1996), *Russia's Regions: A Business Analysis*, The Economist Intelligence Unit, London.

Bradshaw, M. J. (1995), *Regional Patterns of Foreign Investment in Russia*, Royal Institute of International Affairs, London.

Bradshaw, M. J. (1995), 'The Russian North in Transition: General Introduction', *Post-Soviet Geography*, vol. 34, no. 4, pp. 195–203.

Bradshaw, M. J. (1992), *The Economic Effects of Soviet Dissolution*, Royal Institute of International Affairs, London.

Bradshaw, M. J. and Hanson, P. (1994), 'Regions, Local Power and Reform in Russia', in R. W. Campbell (ed.), *Issues in the Transformation of Centrally Planned Economies: Essays in Honour of Gregory Grossman*, Boulder, CO, pp. 133–63.

Gibson, J and Hanson, P. (1996), *Transformation from Below: Local Power and the Political Economy of Post-Communist Transitions*, Cheltenham.

Hanson, P. (1994), *Regions, Local Power and Economic Change in Russia*, Royal Institute of International Affairs, London.

Kirkow, P. (1994), 'Regional Politics and Market Reform in Russia: The Case of the Altai', *Europe-Asia Studies*, vol. 46, no. 7, pp. 1163–87.

Kirkow, P. and Hanson, P. (1994), 'The Potential for Autonomous Regional Development in Russia: The Case of Primorskiy Kray', *Post-Soviet Geography*, vol. 35, no. 2, pp. 63–88.

Shaw, D. J. B. (1995), *The Post-Soviet Republics: A Systematic Geography*, Harlow, Essex.

Sutherland, D. and Hanson, P. (1996), 'Structural Change in the Economies of Russia's Regions', *Europe-Asia Studies*, vol. 48, no. 3, pp. 367–92.

18 Conclusion

F. W. CARTER and W. MAIK

The transition process in the countries of Eastern Europe is highly complex, involving many more aspects than found between the covers of this book. Unemployment and rapid declines in production and economic growth go hand in hand with these traumatic changes The Communist era left a legacy of distorted industrial patterns, an antiquated infrastructure, large debts and a degraded environment, problems that have posed endless challenges for the new post-Communist governments. Moreover, implications of the Communist system's demise are more far-reaching than just economic and fiscal; the effects upon their societies and cultures remain immense. As these countries struggle to find their place in the global system, they will make some impression on the international scene in terms of trade, economics and geopolitics. The interrelationship between the European Union and the countries of Eastern Europe continues to be of vital significance for the latter states within the broader canvas of the continent as a whole. The extent of hopes for prosperity still remains to be seen in these East European countries, although recent progress made by Poland, the Czech Republic and Hungary justifies some optimism. The long-term consequences of a free market will surely bring prosperity to these countries, making any painful sacrifices endured as a result of the shock-shift process seem worthwhile.

The chapters presented in this book make it possible to compare many aspects of the early changes occurring in specific countries of the region; it should be remembered that it is an area with great diversification not only in social and economic development, but also in cultural and historical legacies. It is clear that in future research studies, thoughtful reflections on this part of our continent have to pay attention to the complexity of the area. For example, this would involve an analysis of problems related to changes in the social and economic organization of life, during a period of fundamental transition to the market economy and a self-governing system. Such research could be divided into two sections, namely one concentrating on a theoretical-methodological approach and the other devoted to more practical contemporary issues.

The theoretical aspects of such studies are linked to a need for identification of those elements conditioning the changes in territorial social systems at the local, regional and national level. They also involve some understanding of those elements which determine the role of external/internal factors and mechanisms that regulate changes and functions within these systems under transformation. Underlying this methodological approach is a need to introduce new research concepts; for example, the application of an alternative development model for the territorial social system and its subsequent effects,as argued by Professor Chojnicki and his colleagues in chapter two. Future studies could help create a base from which social and economic policy may be formulated. This could provide a useful benchmark for assessing future research directions. For example, socio-technical categories are seen as an important instrument for local,regional and national policies, which could lead to possible improved working and living conditions and changes in economic and social organization.

The above suggestions indicate a need for certain organizational and institutional clarification. One possibility for organizational answers may come through the continued study of our conference theme in the form of research projects. Finance for such projects could be generated by the Commission of European Communities from within their budget for scientific and technological co-operation between the countries of East-Central Europe and the European Union. Institutional solutions could be forthcoming through study centres that had a multi-disciplinary approach and included human geographers, sociologists, economists, lawyers and specialists in other branches of the social sciences. One potential result from such study-centre activity could be the publication of journals/periodicals and books around our theme subjects.

In contrast to such themes and ideas, it may be contested that Communism's bequest to East-Central Europe impedes any rapid creation of a market economy, and with it liberal capitalism, a 'secular' society and a better organized state. Post-Communist societies may instead develop their own particular brand of social models for which new ideas and attributes have to be established. One such scenario might expect the East European countries to display 'tri-world capitalism'. This would involve the acceptance by some of them of methods and business cultures similar to their First World counterparts, others associating themselves with former Second World methods, whilst those countries characterized by poorly developed smallholdings and street trading have traits and ambitions similar to the Third World. In theory, responsibility for welfare provision and a large public sector would remain with the state. Unfortunately, the state may be unable to render these obligations competently, because the taxed income required — as well as a common belief in the government's sincerity — may be found wanting.[1]

Debates on the future of East-Central Europe suggest a choice between two options, namely the rapid path towards liberal economic and political reform, *or* the slowing down of this change. The latter is a euphemism for preserving as much as possible of the old Communist order. In reality, neither of these choices may happen in practice. For example, in some states the privatization goal is still approved of, but such programmes have been delayed. Perhaps even more importantly, many citizens retreat into political apathy if they feel worse off than before, or are unsure about what can be achieved.

Therefore one may suggest an alternative possible choice. This would involve slow but deliberate progress towards capitalism and liberal democracy. It would include successful new businesses acting as role models for others, utilizing Western investment and management. Emphasis would be placed on educational reform, a gradual remodelling of the professions, institutional legacies would be made effective and other steps taken towards fulfilling possible necessary goals. This would involve a slowing down of the 'return to Europe' process, as well as entry to EU membership in the early years of the twenty-first century. Perhaps the post-Communist future of East-Central Europe looks remarkably like its pre-Communist past. The idea of a 'Zwischeneurope' is possible, with East-Central Europe forming a dependent intermediate zone of weak states, full of national prejudice, inequality, and poverty.[2] However, this is not an inevitable scenario. It may arise if things that must not be done rapidly are done too quickly. The comment of the economist J. M. Keynes in the 1920s, largely with the Soviet Union's transition to centralized planning in mind, was also perhaps prophetic for East-Central Europe. He warned that the economic transition of a society was something that had to be achieved slowly. Keynes maintained that the sacrifices and losses incurred during a period of transition could be much greater if subjected to a forced pace.[3] Certainly the pace of reform in many states of the region has quickened and continues to increase, but it is perhaps still too early to conclude that Keynes's plea for restraint was wrong.

For better or for worse contemporary economists have had their big bangs and shock therapies; for better, in so far as currencies have been stabilized; for worse, in so far as hopes of economic prosperity for many have been raised only to be harshly destroyed. Nevertheless, liberalization and reform are moving forward in many areas. Inflation and foreign trade flows are now heavily influenced by fiscal, monetary and exchange rate policies, in place of the former economic limitations imposed by bureaucratic rule within the straightjacket of Communist annual plans. Clearly, those countries who failed to heed Keynes's advice and embarked on rapid market reform, particularly in macro-oriented stabilization and market liberalization, are at present leading the field. It is now time for specialist advisors, among them geographers, with their feeling for the spatial dimension, to monitor these innovations and help convince the East European countries that all augurs well for the challenges that lie ahead in the twenty-first century.

Notes

1 C. G. A. Bryant, 'Economic Utopianism and Sociological Realism: Strategies for Transformation in East-Central Europe', in C. G. A. Bryant and E. Mokrzycki (eds), *The New Great Transformation: Change and Continuity in East-Central Europe*, London and New York, 1994, pp. 58–77.
2 T. Garton Ash, *We the People*, Cambridge, 1990, p. 155.
3 A. Tyrie, 'Fast is Best for Eastern Bloc', *The Times* (London), 10 April 1995, p. 5.

For Product Safety Concerns and Information please contact our EU representative GPSR@taylorandfrancis.com Taylor & Francis Verlag GmbH, Kaufingerstraße 24, 80331 München, Germany

Batch number: 10725923

Printed by Printforce, the Netherlands